I *MISSED* THE BUS, BUT I ARRIVED ON TIME!

WILLIS L. DRAKE

To all my consanguineous family; specifically my father, Kermit Drake, Sr., my mother, Wylor Dean Sanford-Drake, and my foreparents— namely my grandmother, LA Sanford (Ma Dear), whom I knew and loved. Also, to my grandfather, Joe Lee Sanford, whom I never knew; I only learned some details about him when I became an adult. To my great-grandmother, Melinda Walls-Johnson, and my great-grandfather, Oscar Johnson. I never knew either of them.

My great-grandfather Oscar and my great-grandmother Melinda endured directly or indirectly the hardships and pain of slavery. But their faith in the Lord God Almighty, their mental capacity, and their perseverance to continue with life, allowed our family to progress from their generation to the next generation, and beyond.

Just hearing about my great-grandparents, Oscar and Melinda Johnson, and their incredible story provided me with a personal perspective of life. Just recognizing their inherent personal strength, spiritual faith, and sense of self-worth as human beings inspired me. Without a doubt my great-grandparents were blessed by the Lord God Almighty, and having that knowledge lifts me up spiritually. I know that I have that same DNA. I also possess similar attributes that my great-grandparents demonstrated under much greater difficulties than I have faced during my earthly journey. Therefore, I knew I could succeed in life because I knew our story. What my great-grandparents and my grandparents had to endure during their lifetimes set the foundation for what their offspring would be able to do in the future.

I know within me I can be all that God intended for me to be! By example, my foreparents provided a living model for how we should live our lives. My grandmother, Ma Dear, would always say, "Above all, trust in the Lord God Almighty." That trust comes from faith and being connected to the Holy Spirit!

Contents

Prologue ix

Chapter 1   Mother's Gift of Visions 1
Chapter 2   The Layne's 7
Chapter 3   Golden Gloves Boxing Connection and My
             Brother Charles Drake 31
Chapter 4   The Optometrist 38
Chapter 5   Student at Sumner High School 42
Chapter 6   Working at Peacock Alley 51
Chapter 7   Attending Harris/Stowe Teachers College 58
Chapter 8   Medical Treatment at Barnes Hospital 65
Chapter 9   Refocusing on College 70
Chapter 10 Catching the Delmar Bus 74
Chapter 11 Applying for a Job—Daily Record Company 76
Chapter 12 A Ride with Tim Taylor 83
Chapter 13 Working for the Daily Record Company 88
Chapter 14 Promoted from My Messenger's Job 99
Chapter 15 Working in the Technical File Retrieval Area 103
Chapter 16 Mother's Vision Foreseeing Mary as My Wife 108
Chapter 17 Promoted to Technical Equipment Area 129
Chapter 18 Teamsters Union Organizes Employees 135
Chapter 19 GSA Contractors' Jobs Converted to Federal
             Government Positions 143
Chapter 20 Hired at MECOM 149
Chapter 21 Easton and Taylor Trust Company—Mr. Goodman 156
Chapter 22 Working for McDonnell Douglas Aircraft
             Corporation 160

Chapter 23 Transfer—Technical, Engineering, and
            Standardization Division 191
Chapter 24 Working for Colonel Donald Klovstad 195
Chapter 25 Retired from DLA and Federal Government 201
Chapter 26 Operating MDI (Male Duck, Incorporated) 203

Acknowledgments 209
Appendix 211
Definitions 217
About the Author 219

Prologue

This book titled, "I missed the bus, but I arrived on time!" is an account of some of my experiences throughout my life. Some readers of this book may find that my memory of situations and conditions differ from their experiences regarding fairness in job opportunities and hiring practices regarding African-Americans.

I will reiterate that I am not a trained author, but I know the situations and stories described within this book are true. I know that I have been blessed in so many ways that only the Lord God Almighty could be responsible. It's not that I have accomplished so much, in fact it may be very little in the total scheme of life, but I do know that whatever I have accomplished would not have been possible but for the grace of God. More than anything, I was blessed with a wonderful 55 years of marriage to Mary Ann Byas-Drake with whom I shared three wonderful children—Willis Drake Jr., Monica Renée Drake-Zinn and Kermit Matthew Drake.

As a small child, particularly during my early elementary school years, I remember happiness and joy being analogous to my family and friends. For whatever the reason I always had a bright outlook on most things, regardless of the potential peril. My mother always instilled in me that I could do or become anything if I put my mind to it. There were only a few professional people in my immediate working class community; therefore, few men in my neighborhood that I wanted to emulate. My father was my role model and my ambitions were to be like him. He always provided for his family. We had a roof over our heads, food on the table and nice clothes to wear. My friends always had a cool word to say about my dad; they would always say "Your dad, Mr. Drake, is always nice and friendly to us." That made me proud.

Dad tried to motivate his children to get a college education. He stressed (we considered it preaching) that he wanted us to have a better life than he had. His slogan was, "Use your strong mind instead of breaking your back to earn a living."

As a pre-teenager, I was often asked, "What do you want to be when you grow up?" The stock answer would be doctor, lawyer, engineer, or schoolteacher. For me that was sort of a rote answer. In reality, at that age I didn't have a concept of what it would take for me to become a doctor, lawyer, or engineer. However, what I did have was a father that provided an example of going to work every day. I can't remember that my father ever took a day off from work because he was sick. He was always at home when we were young kids, using the best parenting skills that he had in raising his family. He provided a solid Christian foundation and read the Holy Bible to us often. He instructed us on the right way to live our lives and what he expected of us.

What is destiny? According to the dictionary, destiny is, "The events that will necessarily happen to a particular person or thing in the future." I'm not certain if my destiny was preordained. I do know that years earlier, the Holy Spirit had shown my mother a vision of the girl that I would marry. Also, I do know that on June 9, 1952, my mother Wylor Dean Sanford-Drake, was awarded a landmark Supreme Court of Missouri, Division Number 2, court case decision. Even though others involved in the case were not certain of the outcome, the decision was not a surprise to my mother. During the three-year trial, my mother said that she was not concerned because years earlier the Holy Spirit had shown her this house in a vision and proclaimed that she would own it. The faith of my mother was based on the fact that if the Holy Spirit showed her a vision three times that vision would always come true.

At the age of 12, I met Mrs. Mae Carter-Layne, wife of Dr. Richard Layne, a dentist. I worked for Dr. and Mrs. Layne throughout my high school years. My relationship with them was enriching in many ways; I was exposed to situations that helped prepare me for experiences that I would encounter later in life.

I also learned about hard work, dedication, determination and self-reliance while trying to follow my big brother's (Charles Drake), Golden Gloves Boxing example. I learned about being a team member while participating in an individual sport (boxing). Perhaps the most significant lesson I learned was a defeat is not the end; I can win the next match. These were tremendous lessons in my young life that sustained me throughout my adult life.

As I was stepping through life with the principles that I was taught by my father and mother, I was able to navigate some of the pitfalls that many teenagers experience. This is a rhetorical question, "Was this predestination, having a Guardian Angel, or was it luck?" When I was in my mid-to-late twenties, my mother shared another spiritual experience that she had; although it didn't come from a vision, it did come from the Holy Spirit. She said that when I was born, the Holy Spirit had appeared to her spirit and revealed that I was blessed. She told me that if I lived right, everything I did would be blessed and successful. I believe that predestination is a fact, to an extent, but an individual's actions can affect or "mess-up" the blessings planned for you. Effectively, "All of my mistakes were not God's design. When I got it wrong, He made it right."

Sometimes a setback is necessary to recognize that no matter what we believe, we are not in control, God is. Within a year of graduating high school I had a part-time job and saved enough money to start college and felt extremely good about myself. Then suddenly I was confronted with the possibility of walking with a permanent limp for the rest of my life due to an injury to my right leg. But for the grace of God (it's a miracle) that didn't happen. My college career, however, suffered and I had to withdraw from school that year.

I needed a job and my sister Shirley told me to apply for job at the Daily Record Company where she worked and to be there by 9 o'clock that morning. I missed the bus that would get me downtown on time. Again, was it predestined that a friend would give me a ride downtown, even though it was 12 o'clock noon? Then, beyond all odds, I was hired for the job. Two and a half years later, I learned from the man who hired me (Art McGuire) that when I walked into his office that day to apply for a job, a voice as clear as he and I were talking then touched his heart (spirit) and said "Hire him."

Among the many conversations my mother and I had over the years, the one that sticks out so vividly in my memory was in 1956 when I was 16 years old. My mother told me of a vision that was revealed to her three time; she saw a light brown-skinned pretty girl, who would become my wife. Fast-forward three years to 1959. Unbeknown to me and under unexplainable circumstances (predestination possibly) I met Mary Ann Byas. Four months later I introduced Mary to my mother, who later called her sister, Ethel Mae Sanford (my Aunt Tee), to let her know that I had just introduced her to the girl in her vision from three years ago that would be my wife.

Notwithstanding my mother's vision, I know it was predestined that Mary would be my wife. I also know that it was predestined then Mary would become a nurse for her professional career. Just as I developed determination and focus from my amateur Golden Glove Boxing, Mary had an innate desire to be a registered nurse. Her self-determination, loving care for others, and the support of her mother and father and her mother-in-law, would allow her to obtain her gift from God to be a nurse.

I don't know how to address what some people have identified as my leadership abilities. I don't know if it was an innate gift or if my leadership skills developed over the years from participating in Sunday school and church activities and from my public school education. I believe any gift from God must be cultivated and improved upon. It should not be buried. Whatever the situation was, I was able to display my abilities as I started my first job as a young adult working for a GSA contractor.

During the early nineteen sixties, prior to the Civil Rights Act of 1964, employment opportunities for office jobs for African-Americans were limited. There was discrimination in the workplace that severely handicapped qualified African-Americans seeking employment. There is no euphemism I can use to soften the applicable words to describe the hiring practices applied to African-Americans at that time. I know I've benefited from the Civil Rights Act of 1964, which ended segregation in public places and banned employment discrimination on the basis of race, color, religion, sex or national origin. I personally was blessed with job opportunities that allowed me advancements based on my qualifications and abilities.

However, the practices and policies of some individuals in positions of hiring personnel and supervising employees, didn't always align with the intent of the Civil Rights Act. There was still unfair treatment regarding hiring and promotions afforded to African-Americans on the job. I can attest to the unfair practices and policies, directly and indirectly. I also experienced unfair treatment from some supervisors' personal biases and prejudices. For me personally these unfair situation where few and were outweighed by the preponderance of positive opportunities I was blessed with during my work career.

I believe that the way Mary and I met was spiritually orchestrated and that our life together would serve as an example to inspire or motivate people in positions to effect change to choose to do the right thing.

In 1973, after five years of working for the Federal Government as a civil service employee, I returned to the private sector to work for McDonnell Douglas Aircraft Corporation in St. Louis, MO. I had been working at McDonnell Douglas for about a year when I believe I had a spiritual intervention similar to the one that Art McGuire experienced in 1959 on the day that he hired me for my first job.

As a courier for McDonnell Douglas, I flew to Battle Creek, MI, to deliver a magnetic tape for processing by the Defense Logistic Services Center (DLSC). The processing would take two or three days before I could return to St. Louis with the tape. One afternoon, while passing the time sightseeing in Battle Creek, I had a spiritual intervention; the Holy Spirit spoke to my heart (spirit) with the words, "You are going to live here soon."

Amazingly, within a year (April 1974) I had accepted a job with the Federal Government as a civil service employee working at DLSC in Battle Creek, MI. Again, the circumstances surrounding my getting hired for the job were similar to the situation when I was hired for the job at the Daily Record Company in 1959. I am totally convinced that the circumstances that existed were orchestrated by the Holy Spirit.

In St. Louis during the late nineteen sixties and early nineteen seventies, African-Americans had limited access to homes in the Florissant, MO, area. I lived and worked in the area and, like a fly on the wall, I observed my white coworkers experiencing the situations in their personal lives; some even shared their problems with regard to raising teenagers.

They did not conceal the fact that their sons and daughters were going through the same problems of all teenagers, nor did they disassociate their problems from those of African-American families. Their family lives were no different than those of any normal African-American family. The portrayal of African-Americans families as the only culture or race that experienced the problems of raising teenagers was false.

I believe our entire family had a positive effect on our Florissant, Mo., community. I recall one conversation I had with Mr. Gerald Gilmer, the principal of McCurdy Elementary School where Willis Jr. and Monica were enrolled. Mr. Gilmer said, "Mr. Drake, you and your family have provided me with the example I have been looking for to justify hiring an African-American teacher at McCurdy Elementary School. When I get the normal pushback from my staff when I talk about hiring an African-American teacher, I can now say, "Look at Mr. Drake's family." The second year in the community, Mr. Gilmer hired an African-American teacher, Ms. Dorothy Payne; she was Monica's second grade teacher.

CHAPTER 1

◇

Mother's Gift of Visions

◇

URING MY PRETEEN AND EARLY teenage years, I was emotionally closer and more physically attached to my mother than I was to my father. My father worked the night shift at his job and when he got home from work, he would sleep during the mornings, while I was in school. He would be awake when we got home from school and would have dinner with the family and listen to the radio programs with us. In the winter months, all of us huddled around the warm stove in the back bedroom. His favorite programs were *The Shadow* and *Lone Ranger* and a few others that I don't recall. My father interacted with us in the evenings, and then he would go to bed for a few hours before going to work at night. Therefore, I had more direct interaction with my mother, who was a stay-at-home mom. I looked up to my dad and I wanted to be like him. He was always there whenever I needed him. He didn't express his affection verbally, emotionally or physically, nor did he heap *praise* for doing what was expected of you. He was reserved in that way. I loved my dad and I could just feel that he loved us.

My mother attended all of the activities in which her children participated in elementary school, Sunday school, and church. When I was a teenager in high school, she attended my boxing matches and supported me when I participated in the Golden Gloves Boxing

Program. Normally, my father's work schedule didn't allow time to attend programs or events in which his children participated. During my six years of participating in the Golden Gloves Boxing Program, my father was able to attend only one of my boxing matches. My dad always knew what activities we were involved in at school and church. He would encourage us to do well. For example, he would listen to us recite our speeches for the school and church programs. He didn't critique so much as he would just encourage us to learn our parts and do the best we could. Dad would show us how to put emotion into our speeches, and we would laugh at his gestures and how he would say the words in the speech. He always motivated us to do the very best in school and church programs.

The kitchen was my mother's private and treasured domain. She totally ruled the kitchen in her house. I remember being in the kitchen when my mother baked a cake or cooked dinner. She baked a cake or made pudding once or twice a week. In fact, we had dessert for every dinner meal we ate. Sometimes Mother would leave a little extra cake batter in the bowl, so the four youngest children in the family, Shirley, Jean, Joan, and I would scheme to be the last one in the kitchen or the four of us would take turns waiting to scrape the bowl and eat the cake batter with a spoon. However, to get the very last of the cake batter from the bowl, we took our fingers and wiped the bowl clean.

Mother loved to cook, and she also enjoyed talking when she cooked. She could have a fluent conversation, listening to what I was saying, laughing, and answering my questions and not get distracted about what she was cooking. She would walk from the kitchen table to the cabinet, get some flour and other ingredients for the cake, while still talking to me. She rarely used a measuring cup for the ingredients she put in the cake. As I recall, she would measure the flour and sugar for the cake, and she would say, "I need to have the exact amount of flour and sugar for the cake to taste just right." She would smile or maybe laugh lightly, looking at me when she said that.

She would add the other ingredients to the flour and sugar. In went the butter, eggs, and milk, and she would mix them. She would beat the ingredients vigorously as it started to smell good and look like cake batter. When Mother had put the cake batter in the oven, then she would sit down in her kitchen chair. During certain times she would have a beautiful smile on her face and would sort of look off into space. To break the silence, I would ask, Mother, "what are you thinking about?" She would look at me, still smiling, and say, "Oh, I was just thinking about Granma" (her grandmother Malinda).

Every now and then, my mother and I had impromptu discussions about her grandmother Malinda. The strong relationship between the two of them may have existed because her grandmother raised her. When my mother was young, her mother, LA Sanford (my grandmother, Ma Dear), had to move away from their home in Como, MS, after her husband died. Ma Dear went to Memphis, TN, to earn a living to support her family. The fact that her mother had to leave her family to work in a different state had a lasting impression on my mother. I believe it caused some deep psychological scars that my mother wrestled with into her adult life.

Over the early years of her life, Mother trusted her grandmother Malinda completely. That profound trust usually was the way a mother and daughter trusted each other. Since her mother was absent from their home, that special bonding was lost between my mother and her mother. However, my mother and her grandmother Malinda developed that type of binding trust and commitment to each other. They would share their inner feelings about almost everything. The two of them also developed a spiritual bonding. Their relationship was strengthened by her grandmother Malinda helping her to understand the spiritual blessings that she had been gifted with from the Holy Spirit.

From age six or seven, my mother was blessed with a spiritual gift of having true visions received from the Holy Spirit. At a young age, Mother had a close relationship with the Holy Spirit, and it was difficult for her to understand.

I have witnessed on several occasions when my mother prophesied events that would happen to her children. I use the term *visions* in describing my mother's spiritual gift. I don't know from a biblical perspective whether I have portrayed that correctly. For the context of this book, I know that Lord God Almighty blesses individuals with certain gifts. As a non-biblical scholar, I am hesitant to describe my mother's spiritual gift as being the gift of prophecy, which is to foretell a specific thing that will happen in the future. However, in reality that is actually what Mother did, through the Holy Spirit!

Initially, when my mother was a young girl, her visions were very mysterious and frightening to her. More accurately, from what my mother told me, her visions were downright scary for her. Mother said that she just didn't understand the feelings she had about the visions. She didn't know that they were spiritually prompted. She didn't know if the reason for having the vision meant something was going to happen to the person in her vision. She would seek out her grandmother to console her. Her grandmother repeatedly assured her that she didn't have any reason to be afraid of her visions because they came from the Holy Spirit.

Mother accepted what her grandmother explained that God had showed her favor. He had given her this gift to see things the Holy Spirit would reveal to her for a good cause. To see these special things that would happen in the future was a blessing. Her grandmother Malinda told her she shouldn't be afraid of having these visions because they were being revealed by the Holy Spirit and that was good.

Mother's grandmother told her she should receive, accept, and use the gift that she was blessed with wisely. Her grandmother Malinda always talked to her in a comforting way, as she lovingly embraced her in her arms. She hugged her granddaughter and explained to her softly that she shouldn't talk about the visions inappropriately. However, she let her granddaughter know it was okay to share what was revealed in the visions with the people who appeared in her visions when she absolutely knew the Holy Spirit had revealed the visions and they would be true.

It didn't take long for my mother to realize that if the Holy Spirit revealed the same vision to her three times, this was confirmation to her that the vision would be true. In fact, the vision would happen 100 percent exactly as it was revealed to her.

As my mother got older, she had experienced her gift many times. She had become more comfortable with receiving the visions from the Holy Spirit. More importantly, she also learned to only talk about her visions after they had been revealed to her three times. My mother now believed and knew that the Holy Spirit had revealed the visions to her for good purposes. Mother said she had some visions that she didn't share with anyone because there was something unfortunate that was going to happen.

In just about every way imaginable, my mother was extremely close to her grandmother Malinda. As the old expression goes, she would hang close to her grandmother, always under her feet and she was spiritually close too. Being in the presence of her grandmother meant so much to her, and taught her by example how to live spiritually. She nurtured her with love and care.

As my mother matured spiritually and became older, she learned not to tell anyone except her grandmother, or her big sister Ethel Mae, whom she told everything, about any vision she had. When she had seen the vision three times, she would tell her grandmother Malinda about the vision, expressing every detail that was revealed to her. Without failure, the vision would happen just as the Holy Spirit had revealed it to her. This gift continued throughout my mother's entire lifetime.

In dramatic fashion, (I don't remember how old I was at the time) my mother told me about one vision she had. She was married, living with her family in Memphis, TN, and I wasn't born yet. My mother said she saw this big house in her vision, and it was revealed in the vision that one day that would be her house to own. When she had her vision, she didn't have a clue where the house was located. She only had a picture in her mind of the house that had been revealed to her. What she did know was that she had been given the vision three times. Therefore, she knew that one day she would own the house in her vision, wherever the house was located. I don't specifically know the length of time between when the Holy Spirit revealed the vision to my mother and when she left Memphis.

Mother didn't know at the time that the house was located at 4462 Enright Avenue in St. Louis, MO. She had the vision three times, which confirmed beyond any doubt that she would, in fact, own that house one day. I don't think it was a coincidence that the house my mother saw in her vision was the same house that our family initially lived in upon arriving in St. Louis on December 16, 1940. We first lived in the house as tenants, renting rooms from Mr. and Mrs. Fred Hicks, who owned the house at that time.

When I was sixteen years old, my mother told me about a vision she had concerning me. When Mother told me about her vision, it sort of blindsided me because it was out of the blue, as the expression goes. In her vision, Mother saw a light brown-skinned girl, a pretty girl, as she would say, who would become my wife. Mother knew it would happen because the vision had been revealed to her three times.

Another spiritual experience of my mother's that she shared with me occurred when I was in my mid-to-late twenties. Although it wasn't a vision that she had, it did come from the Holy Spirit. She said that when I was born the Holy Spirit had appeared to her spirit and revealed that I was blessed. She told me that if I lived right, everything I did would be blessed and successful.

Mother told me that when I was only two or three months old, the aura that I generated carried a strong presence. She said my spiritual presence as a baby was so powerfully strong, unlike any of her other children, that she could not get dressed in the same room with me. Mother said that my brother Kermit Jr. was also a blessed child, but his aura did not have the same effect on her.

CHAPTER 2

◇

The Layne's

◇

D R. RICHARD AND MRS. MAE Carter-Layne lived in Lewis Place, which was a private gated community. Taylor Avenue was on the east end and Walton Avenue was on the west end of Lewis Place. The only way an automobile could be driven into Lewis Place was from Marcus Avenue, which was a cross street between McMillan and Newberry Terrace Avenues.

Lewis Place was only two blocks long, and it had beautiful homes. The grass and flowers that divided the street's traffic going east and west looked like a scene out of a picture book. The people who lived in Lewis Place at that time were white. In 1944, I believe Dr. and Mrs. Layne were the first African American family who bought a house in Lewis Place. It was not an easy process for them. They had to contend with being sued under the terms of the *restrictive covenant after they moved in their house. However, the neighborhood started to change when African-American professionals (doctors, lawyers, and school teachers) began to move into Lewis Place. As African-Americans moved in, the white population started to move out, en masse.

In 1941 my family lived at 4472 Finney Avenue. Finney Avenue intersected at Taylor Avenue, where Lewis Place began west of Taylor Avenue. African-Americans were rapidly buying houses and were living west of Kingshighway Avenue. That migration started in the 1950s.

The homes in Lewis Place were upscale compared to the apartment houses on Finney, Fairfax, and Cook Avenues, where the low-income families lived. That is probably why Lewis Place was the last area in this community to change from an all-white community to an African-American community.

Dr. and Mrs. Layne's house, 2 Lewis Place, was the first house on the southwest side of the street. When Lewis Place was basically an all-white community, African Americans couldn't walk through Lewis Place to get to the next street, Walton Avenue, which was the street school children in my community had to cross going to Washington Elementary School. Children had to walk one block north to Newberry Terrance Avenue, or one block south to McMillan Street to get to Washington Elementary School. That route to school added an extra quarter of a mile for children to walk to school. As more African-Americans began living in Lewis Place, African-American children were allowed to walk through Lewis Place to get to Washington Elementary School.

Dr. Richard and Mrs. Mae Carter-Layne's home, 2 Lewis Place

I first met Mrs. Mae Carter-Layne when I was 12 years old. It was in late June, on a Saturday, around two thirty in the afternoon. It was a typical summer Saturday, and just like most summer days, the kids in the neighborhood would play baseball on the vacant corner lot. We didn't have any actual baseball equipment; we used pieces of crushed cardboard boxes for our bases. This lot is where we hung out when we didn't have chores or anything else to do.

I can still visualize this short, heavyset lady, with dyed red hair and a medium light brown skin complexion. She walked diagonally across the street at Taylor Avenue from her house to the vacant lot at Fairfax Avenue, where a group of ten or twelve boys were playing baseball. She had a brown and white cocker spaniel female dog named Lady.

Mrs. Layne walked fast to get out of the street because of the oncoming cars. Her dog, Lady, was on a leash and waddled across the street with her. As she approached our sandlot baseball field, she seemed to be sizing up all the kids. We were in the middle of the baseball game, and Mrs. Layne said, "Excuse me. Can I interrupt your game for a minute?" Everyone stopped playing baseball. Several boys went over to where she was standing behind first base. In a loud voice, Mrs. Layne asked if three or four of us wanted a job working for a week. She said that she would pay us well.

Arthur (Al) Buford asked what type work we would have to do. She replied that she had a house in Pacific, MO, that needed to be cleaned and painted, and she needed help with that.

Mrs. Layne wanted to hire the older boys for the job. I was right there in her face waving my right hand so she would see me. I said to her, "I want to work, I want to work." Mrs. Layne appeared to purposefully look over me to select the older boys. But I was persistent and told her I knew how to work hard, I would do a good job, and I could even learn to paint. Mrs. Layne told me that I was so little that she didn't think I could do the work. I told her, "I am a hard worker. Just give me a chance and I will prove it to you." I remember Mrs. Layne chose my friend Al Buford and two other boys who were fourteen years old, two years older, and bigger, than I was. I don't recall who the two other boys were. Then Mrs. Layne looked at me and said, "I'm going to hire you."

When Mrs. Layne hired us, she told us to be at her house on Monday morning at seven o'clock sharp, dressed for work, and don't be late. She hired a 21-year-old professional painter named Theodore Blanks. He lived in the neighborhood a few blocks from where I lived. I knew Theodore's younger brother, who was in my sister Shirley's class in high school.

That Monday morning, only four workers who were hired showed up to work. That was a good thing because I was the smallest worker and if the fifth person had showed up that morning, I would not have worked that day.

We started out for Pacific, MO, close to eight in the morning. Theodore Blanks, Al Buford, and the other boy were riding in the back seat of the car. Mrs. Layne and I were in the front seat of the car. The drive to Pacific took an hour and fifteen minutes. It was a quarter after nine when we arrived at the house.

Mrs. Layne had a plan, and when we got out of the car, she told each worker exactly what she wanted done. I was excited about working. The house was located at 501 First Street at the corner of First Street and Pacific Street. It was a two-story wood-frame structure, located on approximately one full acre of land, with an unkempt vegetable garden in the back yard. The four of us were hired to clean up the property, mainly the house.

From the back door, I entered the kitchen. Off to the right was the dining room. There was a hallway that led to the front part of the house and to the stairs, which led upstairs to the bedrooms. On the second floor there were four bedrooms and I think a bathroom. There were two bedrooms on each side of the hallway. The master bedroom was the first room to the left at the top of the stairs; it was a large bedroom with a large closet. The other three bedrooms were average size. I think each one had a closet and a window.

The inside of the house was dirty and had a musty, stale odor. Mrs. Layne, with some agitation in her voice, said, "Leave the back door open and open the front door so we can get some fresh air circulating in this house. It stinks in here."

With the doors opened, the smell in the house started to dissipate. There were old newspapers and other trash that had accumulated. Mrs. Layne told me to remove all the trash and put it into the trash cans outside for the trash collectors to pick up on Tuesday morning. I worked like a busy bee because I wanted to impress upon Mrs. Layne that I was a good worker.

She assigned the older boys and Theodore the task of scraping the wallpaper off the bedroom walls so they could be painted. Mrs. Layne's plan was to have all four bedrooms completely painted by Friday evening. In fact, she expected us to complete all the work by Friday evening before we returned home.

Mrs. Layne also pitched in and mostly worked alongside me. She was a very demanding person and didn't stand for any goofing off. Therefore, she didn't allow us to play around on the job, even though three of us were still just young kids. Riding home that evening, she told everyone that she was pleased with the work we accomplished the first day, especially the 12-year-old, inexperienced little guy, Drake. We all laughed. She said it should be easier the rest of the week.

I got home that evening about seven-thirty. When I walked into the house, my father and mother were both in the kitchen talking. Before I could reach the kitchen, my sister Shirley, who had opened the door to let me in the house, smiling, asked me, "Willis, are you tired?" Then my twin sisters Jean and Joan intercepted me as I was walking toward the kitchen. They poked me with their fingers and said, "You think you are a working man now?" As I walked into the kitchen, I started telling them what I did. I was excited, and I told my parents that I worked as hard as anybody on the job today. My father had a smile on his face and said, "Don't try to do too much, but listen and do what Mrs. Layne asks you to do."

I was still hyper from working, and I told my parents that I had cleaned up most of the trash in the house. Then I had started scraping the old wallpaper off the walls so we could start painting. My mother put her arms around my shoulder and told me, "I know you worked hard, and I know you did a good job just like you do around the house helping me." Then Mother said, "So you think you are going to help paint tomorrow?"

Jean and Joan began laughing when Shirley said, "Willis, you will have more paint on the floor than you will put on the walls."

Mother said, "Shirley, you girls go back to the living room. Willis, you had better get a bath. You smell a little strong after doing a man's job today." The girls laughingly went back to the living room.

My father said, "Son, get a good night's sleep, and have a good day at work tomorrow." I got ready to take my bath.

I got up early Tuesday morning to get ready and be at Mrs. Layne's house by seven o'clock. Mother always insisted that we eat breakfast, so she had fixed Cream of Wheat cereal, two slices of buttered toast with jelly and milk for my breakfast. I left the house to walk to Mrs. Layne's house. It only took me three minutes and I was the first one at her house that morning. Everyone arrived on time, and we had the same seating arrangement in the car as yesterday.

We arrived at the house in Pacific and started working. Mrs. Layne demanded that everyone put in a full day's work. She would call you out if she thought you were not working hard or fast enough. It was only the second day on the job and the other three workers had started to get agitated. They were grumbling about Mrs. Layne's constant pushing to get the work done.

We had a scheduled lunch hour to eat, and Mrs. Layne was a very good cook and prepared some very delicious lunches.

Needless to say, as we advanced into the second day of our work schedule, the progress that she was looking for didn't happen. She was not pleased at all with the progress of the wallpaper removal and painting.

I was able to do the cleanup and trash removal work very well. I also continued to help scrape the wallpaper from the walls. Mrs. Layne continually praised me in front of the other workers, and I think that generated some resentment. Al Buford, who was my close friend, didn't show any resentment toward me. I watched Theodore Blanks so I could learn the techniques he used when painting, particularly the window frames. Apparently, I had an innate ability or aptitude to learn from observation. I also had a natural curiosity about most things that I encountered; I always wanted to know how and why things worked.

The mood in the car riding home that Tuesday evening was very tense. Mrs. Layne lambasted the three workers, except me, telling them she was not satisfied with their work effort. She said the slow pace of getting the painting done was not acceptable.

On Wednesday morning the atmosphere riding to Pacific had significantly improved from the ride home the previous night. Mrs. Layne's dressing down all the workers apparently had an impact. When we arrived that morning in Pacific, everybody was upbeat to start work. The work effort was constant and productive until lunchtime. Mrs. Layne reminded us that we had three days to paint the four bedrooms. She directed Theodore to work alone in the master bedroom; Al would paint the second bedroom; and the other worker would paint the third bedroom. Mrs. Layne started painting the last bedroom in order to get back on schedule and finish everything by Friday evening. I asked Mrs. Layne if I could help her paint the last bedroom. She said, "Drake, what do you know about painting?" I told her that I had watched Theodore paint this week and I also had seen my father paint around our house.

Mrs. Layne let me help her paint the fourth bedroom. She gave me a few tips on how to dip my paintbrush in the paint can and not get too much paint on the paintbrush. After two hours, seeing how I was able to paint, she left the room to do other work. She had enough confidence that I would do a good job painting the bedroom. Before we finished work that evening, all the walls in the fourth bedroom had been painted. Mrs. Layne told me that I had done an excellent job painting the entire bedroom practically by myself.

All the workers were able to make progress painting each of the four bedrooms on Wednesday and Thursday. We completed the job before midnight that Friday. As we started driving back home to St. Louis, Mrs. Layne said, "Drake was the only one who truly gave a hundred percent effort, and the fourth bedroom that he painted was superior to any of the paint jobs done in the other three bedrooms." Mrs. Layne said she would do anything to get Drake back home on time."

It was a tough week, but Dr. and Mrs. Layne's Pacific house looked like a new house when we had finished working. The kitchen, dining room, and living room were totally cleaned and everything looked practically new. The windows had been cleaned inside and out, the hardwood floors had been polished, and the carpets were vacuumed. The furniture had been dusted, polished, and waxed. Everything was very clean. The four bedrooms upstairs looked exceptionally great. We had sealed the cracks in the walls, sanded the plaster, and applied two coats of paint on the ceilings and walls. The woodwork trimming and molding had been painted with enamel paint. It had a high-gloss finish, and it made the ceilings and walls stand out like new. Everything in the house looked great.

Personally, I was able to stand back with pride and admire the paint job that I and Mrs. Layne had done in the bedroom. I felt very proud of the work I had completed that entire week. I knew that I had worked as hard as any of the older boys, and, according to Mrs. Layne, I had done a better job painting than the older boys. I don't recall exactly how much I was paid for the week's work; I think it was twenty-five dollars. I was satisfied with the salary that Mrs. Layne paid me. That week was memorable for me, and the work experience was invaluable.

I had always worked—selling newspapers, shining shoes, and doing odd jobs to earn spending money. To have a job for a week at the age of 12 felt very good. Mrs. Layne was impressed with my work ethic and overall ability. She asked me to continue working for her to clean Dr. Layne's dentist office and mow her lawn one day a week. I was ecstatic to get the job! I had learned new skills that I didn't know I had and, as a result, I was going to have a weekly job working for Dr. and Mrs. Layne.

The Layne's house in Pacific, MO:

When I first went to Pacific, MO, in 1952, it was categorized as a rural town with a very small African-American population; no more than five or six African-American families. It, wasn't until several years later that I realized the actual prominence that Dr. and Mrs. Layne had in Pacific, MO.

Over the next five years, from the age of 12 to 17, I worked for Dr. and Mrs. Layne. During this period, I had some positive experiences that proved to be strong character-developing years for me. I was maturing as a young person and influences at that point in my life were very important. The external pressures put on me, as with any teenager, could be important in deciding how my life would move forward. In addition to the normal guidance, encouragement, and positive support that my parents continually provided, I was fortunate to have Dr. and Mrs. Layne's positive support.

The overall exposure I gained from being around Mrs. Layne, more so than Dr. Layne, provided an educational prospective on handling real-life situations such as work experience, social activity, and self-worth. I began to understand that having financial resources helped to create self-determination and decision-making.

There were situations that tested my character and transformed me into becoming a responsible, trustworthy teenager. I worked on Saturday mornings for the Laynes. My primary responsibility was to clean Dr. Layne's dentist office; however, I also cleaned parts of the living area, cut the grass, trimmed the shrubbery, and did other small jobs at their home. When I worked at their house in Pacific, Dr. Layne taught me how to plant and maintain their vegetable garden.

Being a city boy, I had never planted a vegetable garden; actually, gardening wasn't something I enjoyed. One summer when I was 13 or 14 years old, I went with Dr. and Mrs. Layne to their home in Pacific for the weekend. Dr. Layne had showed me how to use the garden hoe to break up the dry soil around the vegetable plants in the garden. He went into the house and left me to weed the garden. I remember weeding the garden and breaking up dirt around the plants. I was in a rhythm, just moving along very methodically, humming softly or singing. For a change, I was actually enjoying gardening. As I was getting the knack of using the garden hoe, I saw a yellow snake with black stripes slithering through the garden away from me.

I dropped the garden hoe and ran into the house and told Dr. Layne there was a snake in the garden. He asked me what the snake looked like. I told him it was a yellow snake with black stripes about a foot and a half long. Dr. Layne was beside himself as he couldn't stop laughing. He said to his wife, "Honey, Drake saw a garden snake out in the garden. He had the garden hoe in his hand, but he came into the house. I told him he should have used the hoe to kill the snake." Mrs. Layne turned her back to me, and I could see her shoulders shaking. She laughed in a more subdued way. My running from the garden snake was humorous to both of them.

Then she told Dr. Layne, "Drake is a city boy. He doesn't know about using a hoe to kill a snake." I stood in the kitchen, initially shaken from seeing the snake, but I was obviously embarrassed because I began to realize that a garden snake wasn't really harmful.

During Dr. and Mrs. Layne's amusement at my expense, I blurted out, "I don't want to go back out and work in the garden."

Still laughing, Dr. Layne said, "Okay, son, you stay in the house. I will finish up in the garden."

Mrs. Layne told me to sit down and rest. She walked over and put her hand on my shoulder and said, "Son, Doctor was raised here in this house, and he has seen hundreds of garden snakes. So it was funny to him that you didn't use the hoe to kill the snake. Don't let his laughing bother you. He understands that living in the city, you haven't seen a lot of snakes."

I felt better as we continued talking; I don't know what we talked about, but I had a comfortable feeling talking to Mrs. Layne.

Mrs. Layne helped to build up my confidence. She would constantly remind me of the many things I could do very well. I don't know if she actually realized the influence that she had on me. I worked hard and did not earn much money working for her. However, the exposure to different experiences was an education in itself for me, and I considered that compensation for not getting paid very much. During the summer months, Mrs. Layne would take me on some weekends to Pacific, MO. She and Dr. Layne were very fond of me and treated me more like a family member than a worker. Mrs. Layne always called me Drake, not by my first name, Willis. She would often say, "Drake, you know I treat you like you are my son."

I must admit, if I really needed anything and asked Mrs. Layne for it, she would have given it to me. However, I was taught by my parents, particularly my father, to always work and earn what I wanted or needed. He said that I should not ask anyone to give me anything that I didn't earn. In that way I wouldn't be beholden to anyone. I could stand on my principles. I would be my own person, my own man.

My mother and father were both proud and supportive parents for all of their children. I was raised in a home where respect, doing the right thing, knowing that you are as good as any other person that God created, and knowing that you could accomplish anything you put your mind to were lessons that were constantly taught.

One of the positive lessons I remember from Mrs. Layne happened in 1955 when I was 15 years old. I remember this particular day so vividly. It was a stifling hot day in Pacific and no breeze. I had my shirt off and was sweating profusely while cutting the grass. Mrs. Layne came out the back door and she called out, "Drake, come on, son. I want you to ride to the drugstore with me."

By the time I had reached the back porch, she was sitting in the car. I told her, "I will get my shirt." She said, "You don't need a shirt. We will only be at the store for a minute." I got into the car without my shirt, and I was still sweating heavily.

She drove to the local Rexall Drugstore about three blocks from the house and double-parked with the engine running. I don't recall what she needed, but she asked me to run into the drugstore and get this item for her. I got out of the car and hurried into the drugstore.

During the mid-1950s, drugstores had a soda fountain shop and did a large part of their daily business selling milkshakes, malts, and scooped ice cream cones to teenagers. I don't recall if there was a movie theater in the town; basically, the gathering place for teenagers was the drugstore. The drugstores also had jukeboxes that played the popular rock 'n roll songs and sometimes the teenagers would dance if there was room in the drugstore.

Pacific, MO, was a very small rural town, and I don't know the degree to which this town was racially segregated. However, I don't believe there were more than five or so African-American families who lived in Pacific at that time.

One previous summer I recall talking to two African-American teenage girls, who had walked by Dr. Layne's house to check out the teenage boy (me) at the doctor's house. We had a fun but short conversation. I asked them what they did for entertainment during the summer. They said they just hung out at their houses. So it was obvious that the African-American and the white kids didn't socialize together, at least not on a regular basis and not at the drugstore.

I walked into the drugstore, without a shirt and still sweating. I didn't have any apprehension or concern about the teenagers there in the drugstore. Initially, I got a reaction from the young adult drugstore clerk behind the soda fountain counter. There were six or eight young teenage boys and girls sitting at the soda fountain; they were 14 to 16 years old. It was obvious that I was a stranger in their small town, a teenager they hadn't seen before.

Perhaps I may have had an unconscious swagger about me. I felt somewhat confident because I was from St. Louis, the big city. Maybe my demeanor was reflected in the way I walked and carried myself. My parents had taught me to be proud of who I am. They always told me to keep my head up, look a person in the eyes when I talked to them, speak with clear diction, and enunciate my words clearly.

I asked the drugstore clerk where the item I wanted was stocked. He asked me, "Who are you?" He said that he had not seen me around before. I looked him straight in the eyes and told him that I worked for Dr. and Mrs. Layne. He immediately got the item that I came to buy.

His attitude and demeanor totally changed after I looked him directly in his eyes and told him that I worked for Dr. and Mrs. Layne. When I was paying for the item, the store clerk wanted to engage me in a patronizing conversation, but I wasn't interested. He asked if I lived nearby in Pacific. I told him that I was from St. Louis. In a louder voice, he asked how I liked St. Louis compared to their small town of Pacific. None of the teenagers sitting at the soda fountain said anything. I noticed there were a few girls who were checking me out, like teenagers will do, whispering among themselves and giggling. I kept my face impassive, paid for the item, and left.

I learned a lesson that day—the value of having a respectable reputation and a meaningful position in life does make a difference, and it shouldn't.

Mrs. Layne's house was approximately four city blocks from the center of Pacific, where the Rexall drugstore was located. I had been going to Pacific for at least three summers now. I do not recall seeing any white teenagers come into the area where Mrs. Layne's house was located, although the majority of Mrs. Layne's neighbors where white people.

The houses were not close to each other, and Mrs. Layne's property was approximately a block square. Shortly after the trip to the drugstore, three white teenage girls who had been in the Rexall drugstore when I was there earlier walked past Mrs. Layne's house. I know that was not a mere coincidence. I was in the backyard and the girls stopped and asked my name. I told them my name and asked for their names.

We had a short, simple conversation. They asked what it was like to live in St. Louis. What kind of music and dances and other things I did in a "big city". I answered their questions; they were typical teenagers and talked in the same jargon or slang of which I was familiar.

Talking with the girls was interesting and fun. That was the most interaction I had with any teenagers during the three years I had been going to Pacific. Normally, I only got to see and talk with Mrs. Layne or Dr. Layne when he came with us.

Although Mrs. Layne was in the house when I talked with the three young teenage girls, she saw me talking with them. When I came into the house, Mrs. Layne asked me what the girls wanted. I told her that we were just talking as teenagers do. They had questions about who I was, where I lived, what things I enjoyed doing. I told Mrs. Layne that they appeared to be nice girls and I really enjoyed talking with them. Mrs. Layne said, "Drake, I don't want you getting too familiar with those girls. So, if you see them coming toward the house, I want you to just come in the house until they have passed."

I am sure that Mrs. Layne had my best interest at heart when she gave me that advice, regardless of my thinking and position on just enjoying the summer and having fun. I acquiesced willingly to Mrs. Layne's wishes and wisdom. In her mind a young African-American boy fraternizing with white girls in 1955 was not a good idea. Fortunately, times have changed.

There was another situation that I recall vividly. Mrs. Layne had a very beautiful home with expensive furniture and Persian rugs. There were French doors between the living room and dining room. I painted rooms in Mrs. Layne's house and the French doors with multiple glass panes. To paint the French doors required painting skill, plus a great deal of time.

When Mrs. Layne's socialite and wealthy friends visited her home, she would tell me how they complimented her on the painted walls in her living room, dining room, and the vestibule. They thought the walls were painted beautifully, especially the French doors.

One Friday evening Mrs. Layne told me that she had arranged a painting job for me with one of the neighbors who lived at the west end of Lewis Place on the north side of the street where Lewis Place ended. She gave me the lady's name and address and told me the lady would be expecting me on Saturday morning to start the job.

After I got home that Friday evening, I told my father, "Mrs. Layne has arranged a painting job for me with one of her friends." My father said, "That was nice of her. How much are you going to be paid for painting the rooms?" I said, "Mrs. Layne and I didn't discuss the price I am going to be paid."

My father told me that I should discuss the price before I started to paint. He said, "Doing work for Mrs. Layne for a lower price than what you would charge someone else is okay, because she has been extremely nice to you over the years. However, if people have seen the professional paint job you do and they want you to paint rooms in their house, then you should be paid accordingly." I agreed with my father's opinion about the price I should charge to paint the rooms in the lady's house.

The next day, Saturday morning at about eight o'clock, I went to the address that Mrs. Layne had given me. I rang the doorbell, and a Caucasian lady opened the door immediately, as if she was standing at the door waiting for me to arrive. I introduced myself and said that Mrs. Layne had told me to come and see her about a painting job.

As I stepped into the house, the lady introduced herself as Mrs. Jones. She walked me through the three rooms that she wanted me to paint and discussed the color of paint she wanted to use in each room. She explained that the cracks in the walls had to be filled and the surface on the walls would need to be sanded before I painted. The three rooms were large rooms, very similar, if not identical, to the rooms in Mrs. Layne's home. Painting the three rooms would probably take me five to seven days to finish. I envisioned that two of the rooms would possibly require a second coat of paint on the walls and ceilings.

Mrs. Jones asked, "How much would you charge me to paint the three rooms?" I told her that because the rooms were rather large and may require two coats of paint, "It will cost seventy-five dollars."

I told her I normally charge forty dollars a room based on the size of the room. However, I would only charge her twenty-five dollars a room because Mrs. Layne had recommended me. I explained that I was giving her a forty-five-dollar discount and she would have to provide the paint and paint supplies.

Mrs. Jones appeared to be surprised and maybe even a little upset about the price I quoted. She said that she would think about it and let me know what she decided. It took me less than ten minutes to walk from Mrs. Jones' house to Mrs. Layne's house. By the time I arrived at the house, Mrs. Layne had come from the living area into the dentist office to meet me. She was furious!

Mrs. Layne said, "Drake, son, you are only 15 or 16 years old now. I told Mrs. Jones that you would paint the three rooms for twenty dollars. You just can't look at making a large amount of money now, but you have to look at what the future might provide for you."

I told Mrs. Layne that I was 16 and would be 17 later this year. I explained that if my work was done professionally enough, Mrs. Jones should be willing to pay me the same as a professional painter, regardless of my age.

These were essentially the same words that my father and I had discussed the night before. My father told me his opinion, and I totally agreed with him. I believe that was the defining moment when I started to develop as a young person, able to express my opinion even though it was contrary to what Mrs. Layne had expressed. I guess I was coming into my own as a young man guided by my father, with whom I had the ultimate confidence and respect.

Mrs. Layne directed me to go back and tell Mrs. Jones that I would paint her three rooms for twenty dollars, which was the price Mrs. Layne had negotiated. Very respectfully, I explained to Mrs. Layne that I could not in good conscience do that amount of painting for the unreasonable price of twenty dollars. That situation caused a temporary strain on our personal relationship.

It was routine for me to approach Dr. Layne when Mrs. Layne and I had our differences. Both Dr. and Mrs. Layne treated me like a family member and I could always explain my position. I discussed my viewpoint with Dr. Layne and he was in total agreement with me. He said, "Drake, Mae (Mrs. Layne) sometimes doesn't think things through completely. That's a big paint job to do that cheap, for anybody, including us. I will talk with Mrs. Layne about this. I am sure she will understand your position, and I support it as being the right thing."

Within a few weeks, Mrs. Layne and I had reconciled. I continued to work for Dr. and Mrs. Lane until I graduated from high school. Before our disagreement, Mrs. Layne would often tell me that she was going to pay for me to go to college. However, after the position I took regarding the price of the paint job for her friend, I don't recall that she ever mentioned that again. My parents always taught me to have integrity, to know my self-worth, and to do what was right.

Mrs. Layne was also an entrepreneur of sorts. When I first worked for Mrs. Layne, she would host promotional and business events in her home. She was successful in most of her endeavors, primarily because of her social status. Due to her networking connections, a large number of people attended these business ventures. She would demonstrate a variety of new kitchen equipment items that would slice and dice vegetables and other foods into various shapes and sizes. The kitchen products were new, expensively priced and not yet available in the commercial retail stores. Mrs. Layne was able to sell many of the products probably because of her position in the African-American society circle. Her various business dealings generated financial gain for her.

Mrs. Layne told me after she had finished one of her sales events that she had made thousands of dollars from that one night's event. That was more than the working people in my neighborhood would make during many months of working on their jobs. It was mind-boggling and unimaginable that the upper-class African-American professionals would spend that amount of money on a kitchen gadget.

The average African-American family at that time would use a regular kitchen knife to slice the vegetables and other food products. The slicing apparatus appeared to be more of a fad of sorts or maybe a stage that some wealthy people were going through. They probably didn't need those gadget items.

Mrs. Layne would often leave large sums of money laying around—in the dining room, bedrooms, the kitchen, and basically anywhere in her house. There would be hundreds, possibly thousands, of dollars all over the house. If it was Mrs. Layne's intention to tempt me to steal money from her, I passed the test overwhelmingly; I never took any of the money.

I was taught by my parents, specifically by my mother, to never steal or lie. I was taught to ask if you wanted something and that you had to work for it. If you don't have the money and can't buy something you want, then you just go without it. Those were core principles that I lived by ever since I was a child.

Introduced to Mary

Mrs. Layne was an honest-speaking person, and this may have been a fault of hers instead of an asset. When I first introduced Mary, my wife, to Mrs. Layne, she told Mary how fortunate she was to have me as her husband. She told Mary, "I have known Drake since he was a little bitty thing. He begged me to hire him to work for me, and I thought he was too small and young. But he proved to be the best worker and young man that I ever have been associated with, and that includes the doctor, my husband. So I know you got you a great husband, and I just hope Drake has in you a wonderful wife."

Mrs. Layne was impressed with the fact that Mary was a student at the Homer G. Phillips School of Nursing. I had talked about Mrs. Layne so much that Mary must have felt like she already knew her before she met her.

Mrs. Layne and I were able to continue our friendship after Mary and I were married. However, we did not stay in close contact with one another. Dr. Layne died in 1969 after we had moved from the city area to Florissant, MO. I didn't learn of his passing until after he was buried.

Whenever we would visit, if she had company, Mrs. Layne would introduce us to them and their response was usually the same, "So, you are Drake? I am so glad to finally meet you. Mae talks about you so much. It's always, Drake this or Drake that. Well, I can tell you that she surely thinks the world about you."

On one occasion, after Mrs. Layne enthusiastically greeted me and Mary with a big hug, she introduced us to her friends. She told stories about the times I worked for her when I was a young kid. She still had that direct approach and serious look when she was talking about something that meant a lot to her. She had her left hand on my shoulder and gestured with her right hand to emphasize her point.

She said, "For all the years that Drake worked for me, I can tell you he never took a dime from me, and I would have money laying all around the house. I was never concerned about money coming up missing with regard to Drake."

She smiled as she talked. She also told a story about the time she had given me the keys to her house when she and Dr. Layne had gone to Pacific, MO, for the weekend. I needed the keys so I could get into the house and clean the dental office.

With her hand still on my shoulder, she said, "I trusted Drake with the keys to my house and anything that I owned." Now laughing, Mrs. Layne said that after I had waxed and buffed the floors in the dentist office, I did not want to walk across the floors to go out of the house.

I don't remember if I had ever told this story to Mary before, so I believe she was hearing it for the first time. Hearing the story again, I began to laugh because I knew what the punch-line was. She said, "Drake decided to go out the front door instead of the dental office door. So, he put the house keys on the table in the dining room for me to get when I returned home on Monday.

"However, Drake didn't check to make sure the outside door from the vestibule was open. He had locked himself out of the house, and he couldn't get out from the vestibule area. Drake was stuck in the vestibule for four or five hours. Finally, a lady walked past the house, and Drake got her attention. He asked the lady to call the police, so he could get out of the vestibule."

Still laughing, Mrs. Layne continued with the story. She explained, "When the police came, Drake had to break the small glass pane in the vestibule's French door." At that point Mrs. Layne opened the front door and motioned for her friends to look at the vestibule door, which was the same door she had back then. She said, "After Drake broke the glass pane, he had to squeeze through that little opening." She roared with laughter. Recalling that story, I don't think I will ever forget Mrs. Layne retelling that story and the laughter and joy all of us had that day.

During the time that I worked for Mrs. Layne, I learned that her family was from Dayton, OH. She was very proud of her family background. When she talked about her family, the Carters, it was almost to the point of bragging. She wanted you to know that her family was a prominent African-American family in Dayton, OH.

Mrs. Layne's brother, Mr. Carter, visited her on several occasions when I was a teenager working for her. Apparently, she had told her brother about me, and when we first met, he let me know how much his sister, Mae, had told him about me. He said that he felt as if he already knew me and it was a pleasure to finally meet me. In later years as an adult working for Headquarters Defense Logistics Agency, I had to travel to Dayton, OH. On several occasions, I visited with Mrs. Layne's brother and met his wife. We always had a pleasant visit, but they were short visits because Mr. Carter was caring for his sick wife.

Mrs. Layne was a very confident woman, and she would always introduce herself as Mrs. Layne or Dr. Richard Layne's wife. Subconsciously, it was important to her to indicate that she was a doctor's wife because it had a certain status that possibly allowed her some privileges in the African-American community. By no means did I find her to be a snob.

On one of my trips back to St. Louis, my wife, Mary, and I visited Mrs. Layne at the nursing home where she was living. At that time, I believe Mrs. Layne was suffering from an early stage of dementia or possibly the early stages of Alzheimer's.

I had contacted the nursing home in advance to let the administration know I was a friend from many years ago and that my wife and I planned to visit Mrs. Layne. When we arrived at the nursing home, the nurse who cared for her walked back to the day room with us where Mrs. Layne was sitting in a wheelchair. All the nursing staff called her "Momma." The nurse said to Mrs. Layne, "Momma, you have some visitors." The nurse told me that sometimes she had difficulty remembering things, communicating, and talking coherently. When I walked up to Mrs. Layne, she had her head down, sort of slumped over in her wheelchair. I walked in front of her wheelchair and said, "Hello, Mrs. Layne." She raised her head from the bowed position. When she saw me, she smiled, her eyes brightened up, and she said, "Drake?" in the form of a question, as if she wasn't sure it was me. I said yes and bent down so she could see me more clearly. I gave her a hug and kissed her cheek. Her eyes welled up, and tears slowly rolled down her face. Mary, my wife, also spoke to Mrs. Layne and hugged her. We visited with her for just a short time, but I could tell my presence had brought a moment of happiness to Mrs. Layne.

As we were leaving, I told Mrs. Layne that I would visit her whenever I was in town. Walking to the exit door, the nurse told me that she was so glad that I came to see "Momma" because she didn't get any visitors. The nurse also told me that she was so glad to meet me and to know that Drake was a real person because "Momma" frequently called my name. She said, "Now I know she has good memories when she mentions your name, Drake." I never knew when Mrs. Layne passed away.

On many occasions when I was back in St. Louis, I would pass by Mrs. Layne's house. My thoughts automatically went back to the times that I spent working for her and Dr. Layne. When I was in St. Louis in June 2018, I drove by the house and stopped. I took a chance and rang the doorbell to talk with the people living in the house.

The man living there, Mr. Alvin Willis, answered the door. I told him who I was and that I wanted to take a picture of the vestibule where I was locked in when I worked for Mrs. Layne. Mr. Willis and I talked for about an hour. We had a very interesting conversation; he told me he had purchased the house when it was in probate. We exchanged information about Dr. and Mrs. Layne and the pioneer-type people they were, fighting the segregation conditions of buying a home in Lewis Place.

On another visit to St. Louis, I visited with Alvin Willis. He invited me into his home and we talked for about 30 minutes. I felt good knowing that really nice people were living in Dr. and Mrs. Layne's old house. I had very fond memories of my time when I worked for the Layne's.

CHAPTER 3

---◇---

Golden Gloves Boxing Connection and My Brother Charles Drake

---◇---

B OXING BECAME POPULAR IN MY neighborhood because Joe Louis, an African-American, was the world heavyweight boxing champion in 1937. Joe Louis's nickname was the Brown Bomber. He was respected by most Americans because he had "stuck it in Hitler's eye." He had single-handedly helped to erode the myth of the master race.

Therefore, Golden Gloves, the sport of amateur boxing, had become a very popular sport for Americans, particularly African-Americans. There were many young kids in St. Louis, as well as throughout the country, who trained in the Golden Gloves Amateur Boxing Program.

I think my brother Charles was 14 or 15 years old when he talked my parents into letting him join the Tandy Center Golden Gloves boxing team. Charles had a very short temper, and he was often getting into fights with kids at school. He didn't take any stuff from anybody.

Charles was the first amateur Golden Gloves boxer from our neighborhood. Not long after Charles started boxing and training at Tandy's Center, a neighborhood friend, William Anderson, asked Charles if he could go to the gym with him. William had always looked up to Charles. William's parents agreed to let him join the Tandy boxing team as long as he could walk with Charles to the gym.

Within a couple years after William had joined Tandy's boxing team, Charles joined the military. At that point, William became the only Golden Gloves boxer from our neighborhood who was a member of the Tandy boxing team.

William began to take his younger brother, James Anderson, to the gym to train for the Golden Gloves boxing team. William's boxing skills earned him respect from the younger kids in our neighborhood, including me.

After training for about two weeks, James became a member of the boxing team. I always had fun being around James. He would shadow box and dance around like he was in a boxing ring.

James said, "Willis, it's cool being on the boxing team. Why don't you ask your mother to let you join the boxing team?"

As soon as we walked in my house, Mother said with a smile on her face, "What are you two up to now?" Without any hesitation, I asked, "Mom, can I go with James and join the Tandy's Golden Gloves boxing team?" Mother said, "Go talk with your father."

James went with me to talk with my dad, and he said that I could try out for the boxing team. My father also said, "I think you just want to do what your big brother Charles did. Go on boy, Willis, get out of here."

I had been training for a week when James and I got our friend Stanley (Stan) McKissic to also join the Tandy boxing team. It wasn't too hard to get Stan's parents to let him join the boxing team because James, William, and I were already on the team. James was 14 years old and Stan and I were 12 years old. The St. Louis City Recreation Boxing Program was scheduled over a four- or five-month period, starting in October and lasting through January or February.

The amateur boxers were predominantly from the St. Louis City Recreation Boxing Programs. The African-American boxers were from the north area of St. Louis. Located in the African-American communities were the Tandy, Vashon, Gamble, Wohl, and Buda Boxing Centers. Also, there were several city recreation boxing programs located in south St. Louis that were predominantly white boxers. There were some good white boxers who came out of the Cherokee and South Broadway boxing programs in south St. Louis.

I was a relatively new boxer on the boxing team and I didn't have natural boxing instincts or skills. Coach Charles O'Kelly was the boxing coach when I first joined the Tandy boxing team and he didn't think I was mean enough to be a boxer. For whatever the reason, I hadn't established a close relationship with him.

After my first year on the Tandy boxing team, Mr. Leon Hare, a former amateur and professional boxer from Saint Louis, was hired as the new boxing coach. Coach Leon took me under his wing as his special project; he spent a lot of time showing me the basic boxing techniques. He built up my confidence. As a result, I became a more skillful boxer.

Coach Leon said that I had tremendous defensive boxing skills, and I didn't get hit much. He described me as an intelligent-thinking boxer. He constantly told me, "I think with those defensive attributes, you could enjoy being a Golden Gloves boxing champion." I was never hurt in the boxing ring. Probably my biggest disadvantage was that I didn't want to hurt my opponent. I just never acquired the temperament.

The most valuable life lesson I learned from boxing in the Golden Gloves was the importance of being prepared physically, mentally, and spiritually. I transferred that knowledge and confidence to most everything I did outside the boxing ring as well. I also learned how to be a good teammate. In the boxing ring, I would always pray that I wouldn't get hurt, that I would win my boxing match, and that I wouldn't hurt my opponent.

When I started boxing in 1952, the *Globe Democrat Newspaper* was the sponsor of the St. Louis Golden Gloves Boxing Tournament (GGBT). The GGBT was held in downtown St. Louis at the Kiel Auditorium Arena, located at 1401 Clark Avenue. The tournament overall was a big-time event, particularly for the young boxers and possibly more so for the African-American boxers. Most of us had not been to the Kiel Auditorium before, or at least not often. The Kiel Auditorium held many of the sports and entertainment events. The seating capacity was approximately 9,000. During the Golden Gloves finals championship matches, the arena was near full capacity. Most often the majority of the boxing crowd were supporters and fans of the south St. Louis boxers.

For me, the GGBT was a fantastic event to participate in as an amateur boxer. The awards presented to the boxers for winning the quarterfinals, semifinals, and championship boxing matches were worthy to have. The boxers received either a very nice engraved medal or a very nice trophy inscribed with the words *Globe Democrat Newspaper Boxing Tournament* and the year of the tournament.

By 1957, the *Globe Democrat Newspaper* had scaled down their sponsorship of the GGBT. That's the year the St. Louis City Recreational Department started sponsorship of the "St. Louis City Boxing Tournament Championships" (SLCBTC). The SLCBTC was held at one of the St. Louis City recreation centers. The tournament's location rotated annually.

That first year, the SLCBTC was hosted by the Gamble City Recreational Center located at 2907 Gamble St., St. Louis, MO. The boxing coach was Mr. Nelson Minter, and he trained two of the most popular Golden Glove boxers in the state of Missouri. They were twin brothers, Don and Dan Edington. Don boxed in the flyweight division at 112 pounds, and Dan boxed in the bantamweight division at 118 pounds.

For that inaugural historic year, the host of the tournament, Gamble Center, expected the Edington twins to be the highlight of the tournament debut. However, the Tandy Center boxing team, under

Coach Leon Hare, cleaned house that year. For me personally, 1957 was the first year that I demonstrated a tremendous improvement in my boxing skills and abilities. It was my third year training under Coach Leon.

My hard training and work ethic began to pay off when I won the SLCBT Championship in 1957. Our Tandy Center boxing team won the overall city boxing championship. I believe James Anderson won the featherweight 126-pound Novice or Open Division Championship. I (Willis Drake) won the lightweight 135-pound Novice Division Championship. Jimmy Miller won the welterweight 147-pound Novice Division Championship. Stanley McKissic won the middleweight 160-pound Novice Division Championship. John Miller won the light heavyweight 175-pound Novice Division Championship, and Percy won the Heavyweight Open Division Championship.

Over the next few years, the competition between Tandy and Gamble Centers was at its peak. Don and Dan Edington both moved up to the next weight class and fought in the bantamweight division at 118 pounds and featherweight 126-pound division, respectively. The 1958 St. Louis City Boxing Tournament Championships (SLCBTC) was hosted by Tandy Center. The boxing match of the tournament was for the 126 pound featherweight 126-pound division championship between Don Edington and me. I loss a disputed and highly unpopular decision. However, I was voted the outstanding boxer of the entire tournament. That was the highlight of my boxing career.

Mr. Minter was not only a boxing coach; he was also a St. Louis City Recreation Department employee. Mr. Minter worked during the summer months at Beckett Playground, located at Taylor and Cook Avenues. Most of the kids in our neighborhood spent their evenings at Beckett Playground from 4:30 p.m. to 8:00 p.m., when the playground closed. We had some legendary volleyball matches at the playground in our neighborhood. We got to know Mr. Minter quite well. He tried to convince the three of us (James, Stan, and me) to come down to Gamble Center and join his boxing team. Naturally, that was never going to happen. We lived in the Tandy Center community, and we were loyal to the Tandy Center Boxing Team. That is where my brother Charles got everything started several years ago, and William Anderson continued the tradition.

As I was gaining some popularity as a Golden Gloves boxer, I began to get rid of some of my shyness and began to gain self-confidence in talking to girls. During the boxing season my popularity was high. This was no different than how football and basketball players were treated during their season. I probably had conversations with girls who otherwise wouldn't have given me the time of day. All in all, I was sensible enough to understand that when the boxing season was over, it would be back to business as usual.

During 1954 through 1957, James Anderson, Stanley McKissic, and I became closer friends. The three of us were tight. We hung out together; if you saw one of us, in all likelihood you would see all three of us.

However, James was two years older than Stan and me and started to have different interests. From a natural maturity standpoint, he became more seriously interested in girls before us. During this time, David Daniels moved into our neighborhood and he and James became very close friends. However, the three of us (James, Stan, and I) still shared many common interests together during the boxing season.

William Anderson became one of Tandy Center's most successful and celebrated amateur boxers. He went on to box professionally for a brief period before he joined the St. Louis City Police Department. William was one of several boxers and individuals who was successful in elevating beyond the neighborhood. He led a productive life and gave back to the community. He retired as a police sergeant.

CHAPTER 4

$\diamond$

The Optometrist

$\diamond$

S TAN AND I WERE FLIGHTY 16 year-old kids and not serious about much of anything when we saw a pretty girl. That male ego mentality was strong at that age. Stan met a girl who lived up the street from Tandy Center, and she had an older brother named Bobby who was about the same age as Stan and me. He was a nice, likable dude. What I remember most about him was that he would laugh all the time.

One Friday evening, Stan and I stopped by Bobby's house. He told us he had a job on Sunday afternoon, and they needed three people to work at a high school in south St. Louis at a charity luncheon. He asked if Stan and I wanted to work the job with him. Stan immediately wanted to know how much money we would be paid. Bobby didn't really know. We would be working four hours, and we were to be at the high school at noon. We agreed on catching the bus at eleven o'clock Sunday morning so we would get to the school by twelve o'clock.

We had already coordinated catching the same bus, so when Stan and I got to the bus stop on Sunday morning, Bobby was already on the bus. If everything else fell into place, it was going to be a good day.

I think the high school was Southwest High School located at Kingshighway and Arsenal Streets. I remember that we caught the Kingshighway bus and asked the bus driver to call the stop where we needed to get off. We had miscalculated the time it would take us to arrive at the high school. From the bus stop we had to walk about a half a block; we arrived at the high school around half past noon.

As we reached the school, I recall thinking it was one of the largest high schools I had ever seen. There were two or three tiers of steps. Each tier had about eight or ten steps before you got to the next level. There were three sets of handrails to the top tier that led to separate door entrances to the school building.

As Stan, Bobby, and I approached the steps of the school, people were lined up from the bottom tier of steps to the entrance of the school, three lines deep and they were agitated. I'm sure it was because they had been waiting in line for a long time. Stan, Bobby, and I were the only African-Americans at the school. We were able to walk through the crowd because I repeatedly said, "Excuse me, please. We are here to work in the kitchen."

Stan, Bobby, and I managed to work our way back to the kitchen area, where the food was being served. When we got to the kitchen area, it was total chaos among the volunteer workers. Because I was in front of Stan and Bobby, I assumed the de facto authority among the three of us. I asked the first person I saw if I could speak to the person in charge who had hired the three of us to work in the kitchen. The lady pointed to a man in the middle of the kitchen area and said, "That's who you need to see, Dr. Ralph DeAngelo, and he does need help with this affair." He was medium height, wore eyeglasses, and looked frantic. He was an optometrist, and was a well respected doctor in his community.

I introduced myself and told him that we were here to help in the kitchen. He simply said, "I am so glad to see you all. What took you so long to get here?" I didn't bother to explain; I just asked, "What do you want us to do?"

He told us he was Dr. Ralph DeAngelo, chairman of the school's fundraiser. He said, "We just need your help. The people are lined up out of the building back to the street, and they are grumbling about how bad this situation is." I asked him, "Can I make a suggestion that might help to speed up serving the food to the people waiting in line?" He said, "I am willing to do anything. Please do anything that you think will help. Let's try it."

The volunteers in the kitchen were parents, teachers, and administrators of the school. There must have been at least four or five hundred people, if not more, waiting in line to be served food.

When I first arrived, I noticed that the people working in the serving line were walking with the person being served and putting the food on their plate. This was a very slow and inefficient way to serve food.

I was 16 years old and here was a group of professional people in distress because they could not accommodate the people in the food-serving line. I told the people serving the food to pass the serving tray to each person wanting to be served instead of walking with the tray and the person to each food station. I told Stan and Bobby to put the drinks on the food trays when people got to the end of the serving line.

Within 30 minutes, after Stan, Bobby, and I started working in the kitchen, the serving line was moving faster and smoother. We began to hear pleasant conversations among the people in line waiting to be served. When we first arrived, the people in line seemed to be hostile and now they were jovial.

The expression on the chairman's face changed totally. He was smiling, exuberant, and engaging with people as they went through the food line. I am sure that the people supporting the fundraiser that Sunday were parents who wanted the best school and programs for their children. That day I also saw a community with more financial resources than my community.

The reason I am talking about this experience is because it was the first time that I realized how some people place so much importance on the impression they make and what it can mean to their personal image or professional prestige.

Dr. DeAngelo came over to me and said, "Willis, I know the other two guys worked hard too, but you just came in and took over, and the adults, including me, just followed your instructions. You have a gift of leadership."

Looking me straight in my eyes, he said, "If there is ever anything that you need, you give me a call." He gave me his business card and said, "You keep this card. This card has my telephone number. You call me if there is ever anything I can do for you." He then said "You may not understand now, but maybe later in life you will."

We were finished with everything by six o'clock that evening. I don't recall exactly how much we were paid for working that Sunday afternoon, but I do recall Bobby saying, "Man I didn't expect to make this much money from this job."

As Stan, Bobby, and I caught the Kingshighway bus going home that evening, we were in high spirits, laughing, joking, and enjoying the bus ride. The three of us had made more money than we had anticipated, and the work was not hard. As for me, I felt like a supervisor because I was giving instructions, and the adults were asking for my opinion on what to do.

Had I known then the value of having relationships with people in certain professional endeavors, I probably would have stayed in contact with Dr. DeAngelo the Optometrist.

CHAPTER 5

⸺ ◇ ⸺

Student at Sumner High School

⸺ ◇ ⸺

THE EUGENE FIELD ELEMENTARY SCHOOL was located in the 4400 block of Olive Street. I lived in the 4400 block of Enright Avenue, four blocks from Field School. The first year that African-American kids were allowed to attend Field School was 1954. The Brown v. Board of Education of Topeka was a landmark U.S. Supreme Court case decision that declared establishing separate public schools for black and white students was unconstitutional. Amazingly, when we started the school year in September 1954, there were no white kids in our eighth-grade class. I don't think there were any white kids attending Field School then, period. Effectively Field School was still segregated regardless of the U.S. Supreme Court decision.

I graduated from Eugene Field Elementary School in June 1954. That summer was an exciting summer for me. I was anticipating finally going to high school. Being a high school student was a tangible sign and the next indicator that I was maturing. I was no longer considered a kid, which basically elementary school symbolically indicated.

Historically, there were three African-American high schools in St. Louis—Sumner High, Vashon High, and Washington Technical High. In 1954, the schools were desegregated and many African-American students living in areas that formerly required them to attend one of the three all African-American high schools were now attending Beaumont and Soldan high schools.

As a student and "Sumnerite," I was proud to attend the Charles H. Sumner High School. Sumner, in my eyes, was the cream of the crop of the public high schools in St. Louis. I am sure the Vashon High and Washington Technical High students felt the same way about their high schools. Among the African-American schools in our community, Sumner High held the bragging rights over its archrival, Vashon High School, most of the time. The winner of the annual Thanksgiving Day football game determined which school would own those bragging rights.

Sumner High School also had the distinction of being the first high school for African-American students west of the Mississippi River. Over the years, Sumner High had some very notable graduates, who were recognized for accomplishments in different areas of expertise and professions. Sumner High School had a wall of fame of the individuals who had achieved notoriety. In my class year of 1958 there were several students who attained notable recognition as musicians: Ann Bullock (Tina Turner), Dingwall Fleary, John Hicks, and Alvin Cash.

When I started at Sumner High School in September 1954, the high school building was under renovation at the main campus. There was a temporary building for the freshman class; I attended Bates Elementary School, 1912 N. Prairie Avenue, as a Sumner High School freshman.

Overall, my freshman year of high school was fun. Although I was still somewhat reserved personality-wise, I was not bashful. As a high school freshman, I had the opportunity to meet new people from various elementary schools that served as feeders of students into the Sumner High School freshman class.

I had just turned 14 years old in August before I started my freshman year. It was difficult to understand that the way I interacted with one teacher would not be the same with another teacher. High school required that I be more independent and responsible for getting to my classes on time and learn how to be successful in my individual high school classes. There was another dynamic that involved learning how to meet and talk with girls at this big high school where I had different girls in each of my classes. Overall, I adjusted reasonably well to high school.

I had an older sister, Shirley Ethel Drake, who was in her junior year at Sumner High School when I started my freshman year. She was attending Sumner High School's main campus located at 4248 Cottage Avenue, St. Louis, MO. It was located in the "Ville," a popular and historic area in north St. Louis. Therefore, I didn't see Shirley at high school during my freshman year. We would talk when we got home from school.

My sister and I were very close. As soon as I walked in the house from my first day of high school and before I could put my books down, Shirley laughingly hollered out, "Willis, how did your first day at Sumner High School go, fresh meat?" Since everybody at Bates was a freshman, you didn't hear the "Fresh meat, fresh meat" call. She hugged me and said "How did it go today little brother?" Being more serious now, she said, "We will talk tonight, and I will let you know the things I think you should do for your classes in high school. You can tell me what teachers you have and I will give you pointers on how you should deal with them and basically what you should expect of them." Laughing, Shirley said, "Fresh meat, I will school you on being a freshman at Sumner High."

Mother said, "Willis, pay close attention to your sister so you can get off to a good start in high school." Shirley, now smiling, said, "Did you hear that? Pay attention and don't be stubborn, thinking you know everything as a freshman." I said, "Okay I plan to listen to your advice, but I don't want you trying to boss me around. I am in high school now, just like you are." We laughed, and I enjoyed exchanging conversations with my big sister.

After dinner, Shirley and I got together in her room and she gave me the rundown on the teachers she had in her freshman year and which teachers didn't play about getting school assignments done. I told Shirley that I would talk with her if I had any problems understanding and getting my school work done.

With a word of encouragement, Shirley said, "Willis, just try to get off to a good start and you will be all right. Okay, that's it. Now get out of my room so I can do my homework." She pushed me out of the room, laughing.

I needed to create the best study habits so I could make adequate grades in high school. My sister Shirley was a very good student with A and B grades. My mother would tell me that I should see how Shirley studied and that I should study the same way. I was not a good student. However, I would study harder during certain parts of the school semester. My grades would suffer during the Golden Gloves time, because I would spend two hours in the evening training and less time studying for school assignments. However, I made decent grades when I truly focused on studying. During the first marking period (September through October), I got decent grades, Bs and an occasional A. The grading system allowed for the grades to be averaged out over the three grading periods, and I would end up with a decent grade (at least a C) for the semester. My mother wouldn't accept a grade less than a C.

My best friend, Stan McKissic, and I didn't meet up the first day of high school to ride the bus together because I had been asked by church members to show Sylvia Ryce how to get to school on the bus. Her father, Reverend Amos Ryce, II was the new pastor at our church. Stan and I didn't have any classes together during our freshman year. However, going home, the three of us, Sylvia, Stan and I rode the bus home together.

Stan was more outgoing then I was, and he made friends with a lot of kids from the Ville outside of the area of where we lived. Stan would always make sure I became known to the new circle of friends that included some of the more popular kids in our freshman class. I think the fact that both Stan and I were Golden Gloves boxers, carried a certain respect for us with the new friends we were making. Before long, I was able to adjust, and fell right in the flow of being in high school.

I attended John Marshall Elementary School from the fifth until the seventh grade with Oree Armstrong, one of my closest friends. Oree and I began our freshman year at Sumner High School together. During the school day, I saw Oree more than I saw my best friend, Stan. Oree was extremely intelligent; by the standard IQ definition, he was a borderline genius. Oree had a very dark (ebony) skin color; physically we were similar in size and height, but I was about 10 pounds heavier than him. Oree would always explain things in great detail. He had a big smile most of the time and a tendency to talk fast; particularly if he was excited about something.

I had a successful freshman year in high school, considering that I got marginally average grades. In some classes I earned at least a B grade, which was above average.

Starting My Sophomore School Year

It was 1955 and I was excited just thinking about starting my sophomore year at the real Sumner High School. A new school auditorium, an indoor swimming pool, and the physical education gymnasium had just been completed. I was also looking forward to being at the same high school that my sister Shirley was attending.

Shirley was a senior that year, and she was very popular with most of her senior classmates and underclassmen. She had an engaging personality and a beautiful smile. To her credit, she was popular with the girls and the boys at Sumner High School. She was a true big sister to me; I stayed in the background at school, so I was not seen as Shirley's little brother.

In a clandestine way, Shirley paved the way for me by letting her upper classmates know that I was her brother. Unbeknown to me, she had several of her classmates looking out for me. I think Shirley let one of her friends, Ellis Ray, know I was her brother. When I had a gym class with him, he picked me first to be on his team when we were playing tag football in gym class. I always remembered that friendly gesture from Ellis.

Additionally, I was getting better at boxing, which helped me as a high school student as well. I made the big adjustment from the eighth grade of elementary school to my freshman year, and now my sophomore year of high school was going well.

The social aspect was falling in place in a normal way for me also. I was able to be my normal self, without having to change my personality to make new friendships. I was basically just a pretty cool and all right guy. I didn't bother anybody, but I didn't take any stuff off of anyone either. Outside of high school, I was able to be with my best friends, James and Stan, who were also cool in high school. James was 17 years old and dating at that time, which was more natural for him. Stan and I were taking notes from James.

I think, from a professional standpoint, the African-American teachers in the St. Louis public school system preferred to teach at Sumner High School. I believe Sumner High School had some of the best teachers.

I know each student had their favorite teachers. During my sophomore year, I learned what individual teachers expected regarding homework and special project assignments. I immediately liked my homeroom teacher, Mrs. Overby, a young, attractive teacher who communicated well with her students. She was my favorite female teacher at that time. Mr. Spicer was my industrial arts teacher, and I considered him my favorite male teacher during my sophomore year at Sumner.

I enjoyed working with my hands building and creating tools and small furniture. Mr. Spicer recognized that I had a propensity for using the shop equipment in a very safe and responsible way. I made some sophisticated items on both the wood and the metal lathes. Normally, to work on the metal lathe, you had to be at least a junior. He made an exception for some students.

Mr. Spicer also taught me how to read blueprints and to correlate my mechanical drawings to items that I could create on the metal lathe. During my shop classes, I created several finely crafted tools on the metal lathe from start to finish. I created the mechanical drawing, developed a blue (line) print, and created the physical item. I made hand tools for my father, and I allowed Mr. Spicer to keep a few tools as an example for future students.

Starting My Senior Year of High School

As I moved to my junior and senior years of high school, I identified with additional teachers who both inspired me and significantly influenced me to do the best I could academically. If I had to choose a favorite teacher throughout my high school career, it would be Mr. Price. In my senior year of high school, he motivated me constantly. He would often say, "Drake, if you put your mind to it, you could be one of the best students I have ever taught here in Sumner High School. You could be an A student if you would study harder. You are a very intelligent young man."

My friend Donald (Don) Brandy was also in Mr. Price's class. Don was a very smart guy and we consistently competed with each other for the best grades. Don and I alternated between first and second place with the highest grade point average in the class. Later, in my senior year of high school, I realized that Mr. Price had indirectly pushed us to work hard in class because it motivated the other students to compete with us as well. If Mr. Price had been my teacher earlier in my high school career, I probably would have dedicated myself to being a better student.

Basically I was never in trouble in high school. I was always respectful to the teachers and related very well to them, including teachers with whom I didn't have any classes. There were times when I wasn't prepared. Most of the time I actively participated during the classroom discussion. I did not disrespect the girls in the classroom, nor did I have many issues with the boys in my high school.

I was never confronted by classmates who wanted to have a physical altercation with me or had a disagreement (beef) with me. For the most part, I guess I was really considered a normal student. I was not a classroom clown. I was always neat and clean when I came to school. What I didn't do was study as hard as I should during the first three years of high school.

Tandy Community Center Dances

During the fall and winter, the St. Louis City Recreation Department sponsored dances for teenagers at the Tandy Center from 7:00 p.m. until 10:00 p.m. on Wednesdays at a cost of twenty-five cents.

Teenagers from Sumner, Vashon, Washington Tech, Beaumont, and Soldan High Schools attended the dances. The dances were very popular, with sophomore and junior students. Some high school freshmen also attended the dances at Tandy.

I remember attending my first dance at Tandy. There were some freshman classmates at the dance. I was not confident enough to ask a girl to dance. It was getting close to the time when the dance would be over and I was still standing around holding up the wall, as the expression goes.

My sister Shirley was there; she was a very good dancer and knew all the latest dances. I wasn't a good dancer; it would take me forever to learn a new dance. At home I could dance okay with Shirley when no one outside of our family could see me dancing.

Unbeknown to me, my sister Shirley had one of her friends, Beneddie Green, ask me to dance. I didn't know what to do, so I just stood there looking stupid. Beneddie still tried to encourage me to dance, repeatedly asking me, "Please, will you dance with me?" and I just stood there. After the song was over, Beneddie walked across the gymnasium to my sister Shirley.

As the next song started playing, Shirley came over with fire in her eyes. She said to me, "Don't act so stupid like you can't dance. Come on, let's dance." We started dancing and I did just fine. She said, "You make me sick. Why didn't you dance with my friend Beneddie?"

I told Shirley that I was just a little nervous, and she said, "You can dance better than a lot of the kids in your freshman class, especially the boys who are out there dancing now. So, I don't know what you are acting shy about." Shirley later told me that her friends said that they saw me dancing with her and that I could dance very well. That gave me more confidence in my dancing. When I went to dances after that, I would ask girls to dance, but mostly to slow songs because I couldn't do the fast dances very well.

CHAPTER 6

Working at Peacock Alley

I WAS STILL WORKING FOR Dr. and Mrs. Layne occasionally on the weekends to earn spending money. However, I wanted to get a job that would pay me a reasonable salary so I could save money for my college tuition, books, and laboratory fees. One evening around six thirty I was in the family room watching television when my older brother Kermit Jr. walked in the house and said, "Hey, what's going on little brother?" That was his normal way of saying hello when he got home from work. That night I had a different response; I said, "Hey, Kermit, I want to get a job so I can earn some money for college."

With that usual playful smile on his face, he said, "Little brother, do you think you can handle a custodian job? I said, "Kermit, I have worked for Dr. Layne for five years cleaning his dental office. Custodial work is something I know how to do very well." Kermit realized that I was serious about getting a job and said, "The custodian at Peacock Alley was let go today. He was a man in his mid-thirties so I'm not sure if Mr. Sandy, the manager of Peacock Alley, will hire a teenager for the job."

Kermit said that he and Mr. Sandy were friends and he would arrange for me to get a job interview with him on Monday. Jokingly, I told Kermit, "I will see how much influence you have. You are always telling me that you are the man." Kermit said, "Don't worry about it little brother, it's in the bag. Mark your calendar for Monday afternoon and be prepared to give a good interview." We both laughed as Kermit went upstairs to his room.

On Monday I was scheduled to meet Mr. Sandy at 1:30 p.m. at Peacock Alley. I arrived at the front desk at 1:15 p.m. and asked if Mr. Sandy was available. A lady told me to have a seat and she would let Sandy know he had a visitor. I had been waiting about 10 minutes when a tall African-American man walked towards me. He was about 6 feet tall, a bit on the slender side, but not thin. He was in his mid to late forties and was casually dressed. When he was within three feet of me, he started smiling and said, "You must be Kermit's younger brother." I stood up and we shook hands and introduced ourselves to one another. He had an easygoing demeanor and a pleasant personality overall.

Mr. Sandy said, "Willis, let's walk downstairs to the club, Peacock Alley, and we can talk there." I could tell that the interview was going to be informal. Apparently Kermit had given Mr. Sandy a favorable impression of me. The interview did not focus on my custodial experience but rather we just engaged in casual conversation. He asked me a few general questions about things that did not pertain to the job. As we talked, he explained the job responsibilities and how to conduct myself on the job. He gave me a walkthrough of Peacock Alley. He was verbally emphatic about what he expected and, in some cases, gave a physical demonstration of exactly how he wanted things done.

Mr. Sandy asked me if I wanted the job and if I thought I could do the job. I told him that I wanted the job and would do it very well. I was hired on the spot as the Peacock Alley custodian. Mr. Sandy stated that he was sure that I could finish my work in four hours. I know that was his way of discreetly telling me how long it should take me to clean up the club. I got the impression that Mr. Sandy wanted me to be successful doing this job.

Mr. Sandy immediately put me on the payroll and paid me for two hours that day. I was an hourly employee, but there was no time clock to punch in and out of work; therefore, I was trusted to accurately report my working hours. Mr. Sandy said that I would be working independently without a supervisor on-site. I was expected to perform my job in a responsible and high-quality manner. I would need to clean up the club each morning, but not the bar area. He emphasized that I was not to go behind the bar where the liquor was kept. I think that was because I was only seventeen years old. I had the normal janitorial tasks of emptying the trash cans, cleaning the restrooms, and other similar responsibilities in the club.

After the interview, I had lunch with my brother Kermit at the hotel restaurant. Kermit told me that Mr. Sandy said, "Your young brother's conversation with me was adult like. He spoke very intelligently." Kermit, with that smile of his now a full grin, told me, "Sandy said you answered all of his questions."

I told my brother that I thought the interview went very well and that Mr. Sandy and I mostly talked about current events. With a serious look on his face, Kermit told me that Sandy was taking a big chance hiring me. The owner, Mr. Al Fine, wanted Sandy to hire an older and more experienced person for the job.

My job at Peacock Alley was the first job I had after working for Dr. and Mrs. Layne and the first time I got paid with a company payroll check made out in my name, and with taxes withheld.

The restaurant was crowded that day and Mr. Sandy asked if he could join us for lunch. Kermit gestured with his hand toward a chair and told Mr. Sandy to sit down. One of the favorite items on the menu was their collard greens. Kermit told me to order sliced tomatoes and chopped onions for my collard greens. I still remember how good they tasted. I had not eaten collard greens that way before. I didn't know if collard greens was the restaurant's menu special for that day and if that was the reason the restaurant was full of people. Mr. Sandy also had the collard greens with the sliced tomatoes and chopped onions for his lunch.

I didn't notice very many white people eating lunch in the restaurant that day. However, the clientele who patronized the Peacock Alley were a mixture of middle-income people from different ethnic backgrounds. At least half of the people who frequented the club and attended the performances were white patrons. Overall and foremost, the people were just jazz lovers.

I finished eating my lunch and said goodbye to my brother and Mr. Sandy. I thanked Mr. Sandy for hiring me and said that I would see him tomorrow and I promised to do a very good job. He acknowledged my comment by nodding his head, as he had food in his mouth and couldn't speak. Kermit said, "Take care, little brother, and I will see you later." I saw the smile on his face as I left the restaurant.

I believe the Peacock Alley was owned by Mr. Al Fine, a middle-aged businessman whose family had diverse and multiple business interests in St. Louis. If I remember correctly, Peacock Alley was located on Lawton Avenue in St. Louis. The family also owned a drugstore, located on Taylor Avenue between Enright and Hodiamont Avenues. I was acquainted with the drugstore pharmacist; he was Al Fine's younger brother.

I would often stop in the drugstore and have a friendly, casual conversation with the pharmacist. He was about twelve years older than me. Periodically, we would have serious conversations concerning current events, issues in the neighborhood, racial attitudes, and how to interact and talk to each other. He had a favorable reputation among the Africa-Americans who patronized the drugstore because he showed respect to his customers. He once asked me about my plans after high school, and I told him I planned to attend the local college. He encouraged me to go to college.

The first week I worked out my daily routine for how to get the job done. It didn't take very much effort to get the club in top shape each morning. My experience working for Mrs. Layne paid dividends for me working at Peacock Alley. After my first week on the job, the club manager and the owner extended high compliments to my brother Kermit. They told him that I was doing an excellent job, and that the Peacock Club was looking the best it had looked in quite some time. Kermit was always proud of me. With that confident smile on his face that bordered on a grin, I am certain he told them that he always knew that I would do a great job.

Things had started to fall in place for me. I finished high school with an academic focus and made plans to enter college. I had a part-time job working at the Peacock Alley, and I was able to save money for college. More particularly, having finished high school I now felt like a young adult man.

My normal part-time hours were eight o'clock until noon, Monday through Friday. Therefore, I had plenty of time to enjoy the summer. The Peacock Alley was one of the most popular clubs in St. Louis that featured jazz artists. In the summer of 1958, there were two very popular jazz pianists who had songs on top of the popular song charts. Ahmad Jamal had released the song "Poinciana," and it was the most popular song played on many of the Pop, R&B, and soul radio stations during the entire summer of 1958. "Poinciana" was the one song that was played over and over at every house party or backyard dance that summer. The song was popular among teenagers and their parents. It was a song to listen and dance to.

During my second week working at Peacock Alley, the Ahmad Jamaal Trio was booked there for a three-week engagement. The music trio consisted of Ahmad Jamaal on piano, Israel Crosby, the bassist, and Vernel Fournier, the drummer. Their album, *Live at the Pershing: But Not For Me*, which contained the song "Poinciana", stayed on the best-selling charts for over two years, actually 108 weeks.

Probably the most exciting thing for me at the Peacock Alley that summer was listening to the three musicians practice while I was doing my job. They would rehearse their music and clean up anything that Ahmad Jamal didn't think was preformed to his musical standards during the previous night's performance. I was spellbound watching them rehearse. Mr. Jamaal would interrupt rehearsal when there was an incorrect note played by the bass player or the drummer. He would explain exactly what was wrong and how he wanted it played. I was fascinated by his talent and knowledge of music. It was obvious that the bass player and drummer respected him and his talent. After their original three-week booking, the trio was extended for another three or four weeks. The club was totally packed for every night's performance.

I worked at Peacock Alley for two and a half months. During that time I didn't cash any of my paychecks until late August when I resigned my job. The primary purpose for me working was to save money to attend college. I was truly focused on attending college and was never tempted to deviate from my college savings plan. I still worked for Dr. and Mrs. Layne and I used that money for my social entertainment. I was financially and mentally prepared to start college in early September. I was excited and looking forward to being a college student.

The last week that I worked at Peacock Alley, Mr. Sandy arranged for me to bring a few guests to Ahmad Jamaal's performance. And we didn't have to pay. It was a gesture to say thank you for doing an outstanding job. We had one of the prime tables close to the stage; we could see every detail of the musicians' performance, including how they were breathing and playing every note. We could even see the sweat as they burned energy creating the magnificent sounds from their music instruments. At the time I didn't have a girlfriend, so I invited my sister Shirley, my friend Stan, and a few other friends to attend the performance at Peacock Alley with me.

Being up close and personal with Ahmad Jamal, Israel Crosby, and Vernel Fournier every day was an experience that I still treasure. Mr. Jamal was a slight-built man who appeared to be in his late twenties at that time. He was relatively quiet, but we would have short conversations just about every day. The drummer, Vernel Fournier, was the tallest member of the trio and was probably about 30 years old. I talked with him more than I did with Ahmad Jamal or Israel Crosby, who was probably in his late thirties or early forties. All three of the men were gracious to me, as I was often star struck, with my mouth wide open. I was amazed at the talent and creativity I was witnessing firsthand.

Ironically, years later after I had moved to Virginia, I had the pleasure of seeing Ahmad Jamal perform at Blues Alley in Georgetown, sometime in the late 1980s or early 1990s. I was with my wife, Mary, and friends Charles and Emma Smith.

I was able to visit Ahmad Jamal outside his dressing room before he went onstage for his performance that night. I identified myself and we talked about the summer of 1958 at the Peacock Alley in St. Louis where he had performed. Before I could ask him if he remembered me, I was amazed when he said that he most certainly did remember me from that summer.

I told Ahmad Jamal that he looked very much the same from the years gone by except for a little gray hair. He smiled and told me I was very kind because that summer was approximately 30 years ago, and time automatically brings about change in all of us. In turn, he commented that I looked basically the same.

We exchanged comments about the whereabouts of Israel Crosby and Vernel Fournier; he said they were not performing with him any longer. We exchanged the small pleasantries about my wife and family, where I was living now, etc. During his performance that evening, he acknowledged my presence to the audience, with a welcome to me, my wife, and my friends. He had a new bass player and drummer performing with him at Blues Alley, and the trio sounded terrific.

CHAPTER 7

--- ◇ ---

Attending Harris/Stowe Teachers College

--- ◇ ---

W HEN I WAS HIRED FOR the job at Peacock Alley, I told Mr. Sandy that I would only work until the last week of August, because I would start college the first week of September. In the middle of August, I gave Mr. Sandy two weeks' notice that I would resign from my job at the end of the month. I thanked him for hiring me and taking a chance on me without any formal custodian experience.

Mr. Sandy shook my hand and thanked me for doing an excellent job. He said, "You were never late to work; the fact that you arrived on time, rain or shine, provided an example I pointed out to the other employees." He was smiling as he said, "Willis, I wish you the best in college, and I know you are going to do well. You are a bright young man."

I received my last payroll check from Peacock Alley a week after I had stopped working. Then I went to the Fine's Drugstore to cash all my checks that I had saved the entire summer. I believe I had earned $300 or $400.

When I gave my checks to the pharmacist to be cashed, he said their payroll office was wondering when I was going to cash my checks. It was unusual that the checks they issued to their employees were not cashed the same day that they were issued. He laughed and said, "You were causing a panic in the payroll office by not cashing your checks. How can you save your money that well?" I told him that it was not difficult because I was saving my money for college. He said, "Great!" He wished me success in college; we shook hands and I left the store.

Attending Harris/Stowe Teachers College

September 1958 had finally rolled around. I had enjoyed a tremendous summer hanging out with my friends and just having fun. I had worked at Peacock Alley and earned money to pay for my own college tuition. I woke up early that September morning full of energy. I was excited; I thought, *Wow, I am starting college!*

The college registration procedure was an eye-opening experience for me. I didn't take advantage of counseling during high school to prepare for the college enrollment process. Some students had enrolled early for their classes. I followed the instructions available to get enrolled in the classes I needed. Several of my classmates from Sumner High School also enrolled at Harris/Stowe Teachers College that day. My college classes started the day after Labor Day.

Harris/Stowe Teachers College was located in my neighborhood at 5351 Enright Avenue. Riding the Delmar bus from my house to the college campus only took 20 minutes. From the bus stop, I had to walk one block to the school. Everything was so convenient. I bought all of my textbooks and paid for my biology lab course. I still had money to pay for incidentals or unexpected situations.

I was in the ideal situation to start college. My parents had demanded, in an encouraging way, I get a college education. I saved my own money, so I didn't have any financial issues. I was living at home with my parents, so I didn't have to pay food and lodging expenses. The college didn't have a residential dormitory for students to live on campus. My parents still provided money for transportation and anything else I needed for school.

It's amazing to realize that you can orchestrate what you believe is the greatest strategy. However, I didn't give much thought about it, nor did I pray about it. I just did the things that I thought were necessary to go to college and to be successful. What I had considered the ultimate foolproof plan was not the case. Apparently my plan wasn't the ultimate plan that was in store for me.

Unbeknown to me, I was on the threshold of encountering a physical injury to my right knee that would totally alter my college education. Ultimately, my knee injury changed my life's course.

My Leg Injury Impacts My College Career

Ever since the fourth grade, I was considered *one of the boys* in my neighborhood. When my friends wanted to play cork ball or horseshoes or go to yard parties or summer dances, they seemed to gravitate to me. I was like a conduit with tentacles that touched and drew the guys in our neighborhood together.

The sandlot ball field where we gathered for pickup football games was next to Beckett Park, located at Cook and Taylor Avenues. When we were young teenagers, the kids in the neighborhood would be at Beckett Playground, Monday through Friday from 4:30 p.m. until 8:00 p.m. We had legendary volleyball games every night. Sometimes the parents came to watch the volleyball games.

One parent, Mr. Jones, Cleart Jones's father, played in the volleyball games every evening with the teenagers. He smoked a cigar, so we nicknamed him Cigar. Mr. Jones added a lot of color and humor to the volleyball games. He would jump in front of anybody and hit the volleyball, just before a kid could hit the ball. We had as much fun laughing at Mr. Jones as we did playing the games.

As we got older, we didn't participate in the playground activity. However, on occasion the guys would get together at the playground to pretend what great athletes they thought they were.

I was on my way home from college one Friday evening about four o'clock when I ran into several friends who insisted I join them to play some touch football. The guys were just going to throw the football around, but nothing rough. I was cajoled by close friends to hang out with the fellows for a short time. I agreed, but I had to go home to change my clothes. It only took me 10 minutes to get home. When I rushed into the house. I spoke to my mother, who was sitting on the couch in the family room.

I was rushing up the stairs to change my clothes when Mother asked me in an agitated voice, "Why are you in such a hurry? You don't have time to talk about how your classes are going at school?" I came back down the stairs and sat on the couch next to Mother. I asked, "What's wrong, Mother? You seem upset about something. You're not concerned about me, are you? My classes are still going fine, just like they have been all week." I had a study routine worked out and I was doing well. Although my biology class was tough for me; I was barely managing to stay up with my assignments in that class.

I was trying to rush to end our conversation so I could get back to the playground. I told Mother that I was getting ready to go play a little football with the guys when Mother said, "Willis, I don't think you should go play any football today. In fact, you need to leave those guys alone and concentrate on school." She sounded very stern. Mother strongly, emphasized, "It doesn't mean anything for you to be fooling around playing football like you are still a little kid!"

As I went upstairs to change my clothes, Mother was still talking. She said, "You should just focus on school and act more grown up." When I came back downstairs, I tried to give Mother a hug before I went out the front door, but she resisted. I told her that I loved her and said that I wasn't going to be out very long. I said, "Mom, I don't want the guys I grew up with to think I don't want to hang out with them because I am going to college."

I have reflected on how she emphasized that I didn't need to play football that day. Perhaps Mother had a premonition that I might get injured. As I think back, I wonder if my path in life would have been altered if I had not played football that day. Without a doubt I know I was capable of completing college. However, I wasn't capable of being successful in college without total dedication to my studies!

I rushed out of the house. When I arrived at the playground, there were five or six guys already throwing the football around. We eventually ended up with seven guys at the playground that evening. We split into two teams, with James Anderson, Stanley McKissic, and me on one team. The three of us had been best friends for over 10 years, so it was natural for us to be on the same team.

James' brother, Norman Anderson, Herbert Harris, and two other guys were on the other team. Herbert was a new guy to our neighborhood. He was physically larger than any of the players and he could run fast. He was probably close to six feet tall. James was our quarterback, and Stan and I were the receivers. We had been playing for about an hour, and the score was tied. Everyone agreed that the team that scored the next touchdown would win the game. When our team got the football, James threw a long pass to me and I caught it. I started to goof around. I would slow up and zigzag across the field. It was not a serious game. We just wanted to share time together and have some fun.

While goofing around, I slowed down and Herbert grabbed my shirt collar and pulled me to the ground. I tried to pull away from him and the strain on my right knee caused it to buckle. I could feel the pain; I had severely injured my knee. Herbert said he heard my knee pop. I also had to hear the smack talking about what had happened. Before I left the playground, the word had spread in the neighborhood that Herbert had broken my leg! Fortunately, my leg wasn't broken. Immediately my knee swelled twice its normal size. I had excruciating pain in my right knee and down my leg. The pain was much worse when I tried to put weight on my right foot or tried to walk.

James and Stan helped me to get home. When I got inside my house, Mother said hello to James and Stan and asked, "What is wrong with you?"

I told her I had hurt my right knee playing football and that my knee was swollen but it wasn't broken. For the first time that I could remember, Mother didn't express her usual motherly concern. She was sitting on the couch when I came in the house, and she didn't get up from the couch. Mother's only comment was, "Soak your knee in some Epsom salt to take the swelling down." That was it; she didn't say another word!

James and Stan helped me navigate up the two flights of stairs to my room on the third floor. The pain was unbearable if I tried to bend my knee so I had to keep my right leg straight, taking one step at a time. I stayed upstairs the rest of the evening. Later that evening my father came up to check on how my knee was feeling. When Mother came up to the second floor to go to bed, she called up to me and asked, "Are you feeling any better?" I let her know that I was okay.

I didn't sleep well that night so I got up early the next morning and went downstairs. Going down the steps, I had to hobble on one leg, taking one step at a time to get to the first floor. Mother was already downstairs in the kitchen. She asked how my knee felt. I said, "My knee was painful all night. It ached constantly. I need to go to the hospital to get my leg examined." Fortunately for me, it was a Saturday and I didn't have school that day. She told me, "Call a taxicab instead of riding the bus to the hospital, Barnes Clinic."

As I left the kitchen to call the Allen Taxicab Company, I admitted to Mother that if I had followed her suggestion and not played football, I probably wouldn't have injured my leg. She didn't say a word. I don't know if she even looked my way. She just kept eating her breakfast. I told her that she had always been right in her foresight or intuition regarding the things that I should or shouldn't do. I tried to explain to her that I did not wanted to give the wrong impression to my childhood friends. I did not want to appear snooty or give the impression that I didn't want to be around them because I was going to college.

Mother and I were very close, and we could talk about anything. I told Mother that apparently I still had some maturing and growing up to do. I promised her that I would make better decisions in the future.

This was the first time I had to make my own arrangements to seek medical attention. Neither my mother nor my father were going to accompany me to the hospital. I tried to cajole Mother so that I could at least gain her moral support. Mother was quite stoic as she told me I could go to the clinic at Barnes Hospital to get treatment for my knee. I asked her if I needed any insurance information, and she responded in a matter-of-fact tone that all my medical information and records were at the clinic. She said, "You only need to give the person at the registration desk your name and address and they will examine your knee and treat you." So for the first time, I was taking responsibility for getting medical attention as an adult.

Seeking medical attention for myself was not the first responsibility I expected to do as an 18 year old adult. I was being thrown a curveball that would ultimately create the foundation, step-by-step, to prepare me to be a responsible adult.

CHAPTER 8

---- ◇ ----

Medical Treatment at Barnes Hospital

---- ◇ ----

T HE TELEPHONE WAS LOCATED ON a table in the hallway adjacent to the family room. There was a chair next to the telephone table, but bending my leg was so painful that I stood up and called the Allen Taxicab Company. It was the most reliable, responsive, and professional taxicab company to use for emergency situations, especially in the African-American community.

Normally, the Allen Taxicab dispatcher would have a taxicab at your house in five or ten minutes. However, on this Saturday, I waited for 20 minutes for a taxicab to arrive at my house. It would be faster to walk to the corner of my street and hail a taxicab. I was in excruciating pain, but I decided to walk to the corner of Taylor and Enright Avenues and hail a taxicab. I wanted to get to the hospital as fast as I could. I thought if I could not catch a taxicab, I would take the bus to the hospital. When I got to the corner, I was able to hail a taxicab immediately. Still in pain, I got in the back seat of the taxicab and put my right leg across the seat to keep it straight so I didn't have to bend my knee.

The taxi driver asked how I hurt my leg. When I told him, he started giving me friendly advice. He said, "Young blood, you may have to give up playing sandlot football, man. I am 29 years old, and at some point I realized those sandlot games were child's play and I gave it up."

The ride to Barnes's Clinic took about 15 minutes. During that time, the cab driver discussed life's lessons and his valued perspective on what to do and what not to do. I appreciated his interest in trying to pass on advice to a young brother, but my leg was in great pain and I don't think I fully heard the points he was trying to make. When we arrived at the clinic, he helped me out of the cab so I didn't have to bend my knee. I was able to walk into the clinic without any assistance. Barnes Clinic, located at 660 South Euclid Avenue, St. Louis, MO, was associated with the local **Washington University School of Medicine**. Barnes was a teaching hospital and clinical institution; the medical staff consisted of many student doctors and interns.

This would be the first time I had to go through the clinic's registration process by myself. I was 18 years old, legally an adult. I didn't need my parents with me to receive medical attention. The clinic had my basic personal and insurance information on file.

Generally, the wait time to see a doctor in the clinic could be very lengthy. However, the medical staff who admitted me realized that I was in considerable pain. As soon as I completed the registration process, I was put into a wheelchair with my leg extended outward. I still couldn't bend my knee without having severe pain.

The medical attendant poked and prodded at my knee. Different people kept asking the same questions over and over. I said to myself, "Willis, be cool. Act like an adult and handle your business."

I had become somewhat apprehensive and perhaps frightened as I waited to get medical treatment for my knee. I sat in the clinic's waiting room and prayed. I didn't immediately see the doctor approaching me because I was in a moment of prayerful solitude. He was about 29 years old. He came into the examination room and asked me what happened. I described the physical force from being pulled down from behind by my shirt collar that injured my knee.

I don't recall the doctor's name, but we immediately seemed to click very comfortably with each other. After he examined my knee and had x-rays taken, he diagnosed my injury as a severely strained knee joint. There were no broken bones. The recommended treatment was to immobilize my leg so I could not bend my knee.

The doctor put a full-length cast on my right leg, from my ankle to my upper thigh. I would need to keep the cast on for six weeks. He told me I could go to school but to keep as much weight off my right leg as possible. The nurse brought me a pair of crutches and the doctor showed me how to walk with them. Initially, it felt strange walking with the crutches, especially getting on and off the bus. However, I thought this was just a minor issue, compared to getting around the college campus. I had two days to become comfortable with my crutches before going to school on Monday morning. I would take every opportunity to maneuver up and down the stairs in the house and balance myself carrying my books. This would help me getting to my classes easier.

I had to leave my house earlier because I needed additional time to walk from the bus stop to the college to be on time for my first class.

Because my mobility was restricted, it was difficult to navigate the crowded hallways and maneuver up and down the stairs. As time passed, I became frustrated because academically I was falling behind in my classes.

In addition, it was difficult to study at home because getting to my bedroom on the third floor was a problem; it was not easy to take my books to my room using my crutches. Greater frustration set in and my mind-set was affected. I couldn't concentrate and stay focused the way I needed to, in order to be successful in college.

I did not discuss my situation with my parents. It was routine for me to tell them that everything was fine.

Six weeks later, I returned to Barnes's Clinic for my checkup. I expected to have the cast removed from my leg and be able to walk normal again without any problems.

The doctor cut the cast off my leg. Jokingly I told him to be careful because I didn't want him to accidentally cut off my leg. The doctor, nurse, and I laughed at my joke. After the doctor removed the cast, he examined my knee. and asked if I felt pain when he pressed on my knee. He asked me to sit up and swing my right leg to the side of the examination table and bend my knee. I tried to bend my knee, but the pain was as excruciating as it was a month earlier. I still couldn't bend my knee.

After more tests and examinations, the doctor said that I had a torn cartilage in my knee. I could tell from his facial expression and demeanor that he was shaken by the test results. He told me that it would require an operation to remove the torn cartilage and that I would have a permanent limp for the rest of my life.

Within a week, I returned to the clinic for the operation on my knee. I prayed to God to heal my knee!

I remember very clearly talking to my doctor before the operation. He explained that the operation would take about two hours. He was certain the procedure would go well and told me not to worry. I remember being given anesthesia, feeling drowsy while counting from one to one hundred, and falling asleep before I was transported to the operating room.

The next thing I remember was seeing my doctor at my bedside with a big smile on his face. He explained that when he put me on the operating table under anesthesia, he could bend my knee freely and with total flexibility. He could move my leg up and down and twist it in and out. There was no indication of blockage in my knee. In fact, the doctor said that he decided not to operate on my knee because medically there was nothing wrong. He further stated that because I was so young, he was thankful that he didn't have to operate on my knee.

I had prayed to God to heal my knee. I knew that I had a physical injury to my knee, but I always accepted that it was a miracle that I didn't need an operation and that I would not have to walk with a limp the rest of my life.

The doctor recommended physical therapy to rehabilitate my knee. I met with a physical therapist, who demonstrated exercises that would strengthen my thigh and leg muscles so that I could bend my knee normally. The rehabilitation process was very painful. I followed that routine for weeks without any major improvement in bending my knee. I was still using my crutches to get around at school and home.

I had a follow-up appointment with my doctor and physical therapist, and there was no appreciable improvement in my ability to bend my knee. I was instructed to continue with the physical therapy, enduring as much pain as I could, to strengthen my thigh, knee, and leg muscles.

When I returned home from the doctor's office, I was emotionally down because I still couldn't bend my right knee correctly without pain. As I went up the stairs to my bedroom, a thought came to me about the old super eight projector that I had in my bedroom closet. I think it belonged to my brother Charles. It came to my mind to use it as a weight to strengthen my leg and knee. Although this was unconventional, it worked.

The super eight projector was made of cast iron, and it had a handle on it. I put an old pants belt through the handle of the projector. Then I slipped the loop over my right foot as a method to raise and lower the projector. I used this made-up weight contraption daily. I used the same concept that the physical therapist had instructed me to use. This was an extremely painful exercise routine, but I stuck with it. I was determined to bend my knee correctly again. I felt that Lord God Almighty had blessed me by not requiring an operation and I needed to do my part. I exercised my leg anytime I had a spare moment. Eventually, I was able to build up my thigh and leg muscles so I could bend my knee in both a downward and upward position.

After approximately two months, I regained full strength in my right knee, leg, and thigh muscles. I could walk, run, and ultimately do things that I had previously done, including going to the Tandy Center and training for the Golden Gloves boxing team again.

CHAPTER 9

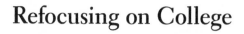

Refocusing on College

D URING THE PROCESS OF REHABILITATION, my academic efforts in school suffered severely. I couldn't maintain the required grades I needed to stay in college. Therefore, with a strong suggestion from the Dean of Education, I decided to withdraw from college. Withdrawing from school left me with a hollow feeling. I was disappointed in myself; I felt like a failure. I was embarrassed and unsure how my parents would feel about my withdrawal from school and because I didn't do my very best.

I knew I would be able to collect myself and planned to get a job as soon as possible. I also planned to go back to college to finish my education.

Withdrawing from school was not the first problem I had to deal with; facing my parents was the larger issue for me. Basically I had always been truthful and straightforward with my parents, but after I withdrew from school, I kept up the charade for several weeks before I was forced to let my mother and father know that I was no longer attending college.

When my parents, mostly my mother, would ask how I was doing in school, my standard reply was, "I am doing fine." Eating at my core beliefs was the fact that I was being deceitful to my parents. In effect,

I was lying to them while looking them straight in their eyes. Lying to my parents made me feel like I was soiled.

My oldest sister, Maudean, confronted me about school. She told me the Dean of Education had called the house and told her that I missed two important classes in which I needed passing grades to complete the semester. She told me to tell Mom and Dad about my school situation immediately. My sister didn't say that she would tell my parents if I didn't tell them. Maudean told me what I should do, and there was no question about it. That was the best advice that my big sister ever gave me.

Deceiving my parents was a tremendous burden on me. That evening after my mother got home from work and had eaten her dinner, I asked if she had a minute to talk to me about school. Mother had a look on her face, as if she already knew my situation. I told her that I had not done well in school, particularly after I had injured my leg. I said that I hoped she was not too disappointed in me. She did not interrupt me while I was talking.

Mother was obviously disappointed, but she was normally even-handed and could see a positive side of everything. She told me not to become discouraged because I would have opportunities in life to get it right. She mentioned that God had a plan for me and that I should trust in the Lord to show me the way. Mother further explained that she knew I had the ability to earn my college degree if I put my mind to do it. She believed that I was one of her smartest children and I always worked hard and was successful in everything I did.

I thanked Mother for having confidence in me. I told her that I would talk to Dad the following day. After talking to Mother, my mind was clear and I didn't feel the mental burden any longer.

Whenever I wanted to relax, I would retreat to my bedroom and listen to my jazz music. I had albums by Miles Davis, Dave Brubeck, John Coltrane, Cannonball Adderley, and Ahmad Jamaal, just to name a few. I felt like listening to Dave Brubeck, so I played the album "Time Out" and I listened to my favorite song on the album, "Take Five," over and over. I finally went to bed and had a restful night's sleep.

I got up early the next morning and went downstairs to talk to my father. He was in the kitchen having a cup of coffee. I said, "Good morning" as I walked into the kitchen. Dad and I exchanged a few words about the weather, how are you doing, etc. I knew Mother had talked to him about everything.

Sitting down at the table, I told Dad, "I did not do well in school, and I think it was mainly because of my leg injury. Therefore, I couldn't keep my grades up and I had to withdraw from college. I hope you aren't too disappointed in me."

I would describe my father as a matter-of-fact type person. He didn't get overly excited about most things. He always seemed to keep an even temperament, and he approached everything in a rational and logical way. In his normal soft-spoken manner, he told me that he believed everything would work out for me and that I should think about going back in college. He said I should start looking for a job to earn a living for myself. I thanked my dad and we sat there and talked while he finished his coffee.

After talking to both of my parents, I felt as if a tremendous weight was lifted from me. I had always accepted responsibility for anything I did, so it was emotionally tough and conflicting for me to not tell my parents about my situation. I know those emotions and feelings were based on my principles and core values of being truthful most of my young life.

I was now in a new phase of my life. In April 1959, during the second semester of my freshman school year, I withdrew from college. Not only was I disappointed in myself, I was also feeling sorry for myself. I needed to reestablish myself academically to be prepared to go back to college the following school year. Thanks to my sister Maudean, I was back on track shouldering my responsibilities. After talking with my parents, I knew that the next thing I had to do was to get a job. The rule in my parents' home was if you lived in their house, you would either attend school, or you would get a job to support yourself. Otherwise you would find some other place to live. Doing nothing or being unproductive was not an option in my parents' household or for me.

CHAPTER 10

Catching the Delmar Bus

I FELT LIKE I WAS FACING a monumental life crisis and I was only 18 years old. Thoughts were pulsating in my head as I rushed from my house and up the street to Taylor Avenue. I had to catch the Delmar bus at eight o'clock and then transfer to the Twelfth Street bus to be in downtown St. Louis by eight thirty in the morning. That critical connection, from the Delmar bus to the downtown Twelfth Street bus, was paramount for me being at the Mart Building before nine o'clock.

I was fixated on the fact that I shouldn't be late. That thought had permeated my mind the night before. And as I rushed out of the house that morning, I kept thinking, *Willis, be on time. Don't be late. Your first impression will be important.* I was sort of just regurgitating my sister Shirley's words. My sister Shirley had repeatedly emphasized that it was critical for me to be at the Mart Building before nine o'clock.

Given the book's title, *I Missed the Bus, but I Arrived on Time,* may appear to be an oxymoron. If not, one apparently would know that the title of the book suggests it is a contradiction itself. In my specific case, it was me getting to the Mart Building in downtown St. Louis by nine o'clock. What earthly circumstances could justify missing my transportation, the bus? Ultimately, I did miss the bus that would have assured my arrival at the Mart Building at nine o'clock.

So how could I possibly arrive on time for my nine o'clock appointment? Again, the power of the Holy Spirit got me to where I was supposed to be and "on time."

The phrase, *I Missed the Bus, but I Arrived on Time*, is more than a metaphor because it actually happened. I am convinced that a series of spiritual events happened that day when I missed the bus. My best friend Stan delayed me from leaving his house several times before Tim Taylor drove by his house. I know it was not a coincidence that Tim drove by Stan's house at that time. Tim was scheduled to go to the St. Louis Police Academy that afternoon, which was located across the street from the Mart Building. Without much effort, Tim convinced me to ride with him to the Mart Building. This series of events allowed me to be in the precise place, at the precise time I was supposed to be there. Therefore, it was not that I missed the bus. Rather, it was that I arrived on time in accordance with God's plan!

What happened that afternoon convinced me that regardless of how much planning we human beings do, we cannot disrupt God's plans. My sister Shirley strongly emphasized that I be at the Mart Building by nine o'clock. I believe it was God's plan that I miss the bus; it was no mistake that I did not get to the Mart Building by nine o'clock. Arriving at noon was not too late; it was on time according to His plan. Mr. Arthur (Art) McGuire was in the personnel office by himself when I arrived. I believe that was by design.

CHAPTER 11

Applying for a Job—Daily Record Company

I T WAS MID-APRIL 1959. MY sister Shirley was working for the Daily Record Company (DRC), a General Services Administration (GSA) government contractor. She said, "I don't know if the company has any job openings now, but they do seem to hire people regularly." Shirley always told me what to do and it was usually the right thing for me. She told me to apply for a job at DRC.

After letting me know about the job at DRC, she emphasized very strongly to be at the personnel office by nine o'clock. She repeatedly said, "Don't you be late, Willis. You hear me?" Shirley was two years older than me, and always acted like my big sister. That was the case when we were kids and as teenagers in high school. To a degree, that continued into our adulthood. She always had my best interest at heart.

She had that big sister's look in her eyes. She said, "You don't know her, but my coworker Ina Boon is a stickler for us (African-Americans) showing up on time to apply for a job. Ina is always saying that when she raises the question of why there are not more African-Americans being hired, the personnel manager would answer that people are showing up late to apply for a job.

The Daily Record Company was awarded the GSA contract to provide services to the United States Army Materiel Command (USAMC). The company had office space in the Mart Building, located at Twelfth and Spruce Streets in downtown St. Louis.

The temperature that morning was reasonably warm. I was casually dressed for putting in a job application. I looked presentable and businesslike.

In 1959, as my sister had reinforced, there were certain standards associated with job hunting, particularly for African-Americans. It was customary to apply for a job early in the morning by nine o'clock.

In the African-American community, often the mind-set was that if you would arrive to put in a job application after nine o'clock in the morning, the personnel representatives possibly would not take you seriously about wanting a job. I grew up having a very strong work ethic. My mother would always tell all her children, "Whatever you do in life, be the best that you can be doing it."

Shirley usually left the house about seven o'clock in the morning to be at work before eight o'clock. That morning before she left the house, she knocked on my door and asked if I was awake. I called out, "Yes, I'm awake, thank you."

As she was leaving the house she said, "Remember, get there on time. Good luck and have a good day."

I don't remember if I fell back to sleep, but I ended up rushing out of the house. I was ten minutes late getting to the bus stop to catch the Delmar bus. The traffic on Delmar that morning was horrific, particularly going east. I couldn't cross the street to catch the bus before it left the bus stop.

I signaled and waved my hand frantically to the bus driver. I am certain that he saw me signaling and calling for him to wait for me. Regardless of my valiant efforts, the bus driver ignored my desperate pleading for him to wait. I was somewhat upset at the bus driver, instead of being upset at myself.

As the bus pulled off, I knew it would be 15 minutes before the next eastbound Delmar bus would arrive and getting to the Mart Building by nine o'clock was very unlikely. I was frustrated because I had *missed the bus.* But I think that most of my frustration may have been the totality of not being in school and being uncertain about my future.

Therefore, with the infinite wisdom of an 18 year old, I decided not to apply for a job at the Mart Building that morning. I caught the westbound Delmar bus at 8:20 a.m. to go to my best friend Stanley (Stan) McKissic's house. He lived in the 5300 block of Northland Avenue.

When I got on the Delmar bus, it was almost full. Apparently, at that time of morning people were going to school or work, or getting off work from a night shift. I paid my bus fare and walked toward the rear of the bus. There were one or two empty seats available but I didn't sit down; I was still mentally hyper because I had missed the bus going downtown. Also, it would only take about ten minutes to reach Union Boulevard where I had to transfer to the Union bus.

When I got on the Union bus, I sat in a seat on the right-hand side near the front. My mind was still preoccupied mainly from having missed the earlier bus! The people on the bus were talking, laughing, and socializing. However, I was able to tune out everything around me. My mind was swirling. I was having difficulty getting focused on where I was in my life.

Somehow, I was able to reach deep into my soul to find solace. At that precise moment of penetrating my core, I was able to focus mentally on who I was and what direction I wanted to go in my life. I was now able to isolate my thoughts completely, and the impulse to intuitively search my roots and spiritually connect to my ancestors gave me a realization of exactly where I was with my life at this point.

Reaching a state of calmness, I began to understand my connection to my ancestors, specifically my grandmother, Ma Dear. Spiritually I identified my connection to my mother and her "gift" of visions. In this short space of time, I recognized a change taking place in me. I now was a young adult, no longer a child. This revelation gave me a momentary pause to digest what my parents expected of me. Also, I needed to understand how my mother's faith had allowed her to trust in the Lord God Almighty and move to a new city, St. Louis, with her husband and family without any reservations. Faith was what I needed at that moment.

I dove deeper into my spiritual inner self as I rode on the bus with a clear mind. I also was able to appreciate the strength of my grandmother, LA Johnson-Sanford, and what she had come through in her lifetime. She had endured her life's trials by being sustained by these words: "Just trust in the Lord God Almighty." I could recount what I had heard through the years of what my great-grandfather Oscar Johnson and my great-grandmother Malinda Walls-Johnson had been through. They were able to endure and survive many obstacles during their lifetime with that same faith of loving and trusting in the Lord God Almighty. They taught their children the importance of this faith. This teaching continues today within our family; it is passed down to their children and grandchildren. Now I only had to absorb and use the strength within me that was passed down to me through my ancestors.

All of a sudden, it seemed like I had awakened from a deep sleep and was now back in the present time. My mind was alert and I could hear the chatter around me. I appeared to have a new awareness, or maybe an increased confidence within me. I'm not certain why I had that feeling of assurance. Maybe I had subconsciously penetrated into a spiritual area during my mental reflection and search of my ancestors' background. Regardless, I was no longer concerned that I had missed the bus. I knew there would be another opportunity for me to apply for the job my sister Shirley had told me about.

I was aware that the bus was half empty and I was only minutes from Stan's house. Now, I was going to hang out with my best friend, Stan and have fun just being carefree and shooting the breeze, as always.'

Stan was just two months older, but he always wanted to play the big brother role with me. Normally I was the more mature-thinking and levelheaded one. That had always been the situation since we were young kids. There wasn't anything that Stan and I didn't talk about. As young, cool dudes, we had an opinion on everything and would defy anyone to say we didn't have the factual answers to all the problems. Regardless of the situation or circumstance, we analyzed all aspects of our young lives, including the good and the bad about everything we had to deal with. We didn't complain about much. We realized that overall we were fortunate in many ways and blessed compared to many of our friends. We came from loving parents and a caring family of sisters and brothers.

I believe a spiritual person can relate to the circumstance I am describing. I believe if there is something that God has in store for you, it will happen within his plan. You must do what you are supposed to do, but if you don't take care of your business, God will step in. He won't let you mess up his plan, if He so chooses.

In my case, I missed the bus and an excellent opportunity for getting an office job, which was rare for African-American teenagers. That was on me! But that wasn't the end of the story, because the question was, what was God's plan for me? Also, if God intended that I be somewhere at a certain place and time, it would happen just as He had planned. Regardless, if an individual (me) takes intervening actions, intentional or by accident, that might deviate from God's plan, He will make sure that whatever His plan is, it will happen.

I believe the presence of the Holy Spirit (God's will) had entered into this sequence of events. This is what I truly believe happened to me on that particular day when I *missed the bus*. This was a perfect opportunity for the Holy Spirit to demonstrate who was in control of my life and my future opportunities!

I rang the doorbell when I got to Stan's house, and when he answered the door, the first words that came out of Stan's mouth were, "What's up, Lumps?" Not many people knew that nickname for me. "Lumps" was attached to me when I was about nine or ten years old. I was always chubby growing up, more so than any of my friends, so the nickname "Lumps" applied. Stan and another close friend, Garland Greer, were the only friends from our old neighborhood who still called me Lumps. Stan was smiling, or more like grinning, as he opened the front door.

We shook hands, and Stan said, "Man, I am glad you stopped by. Come on in."

So many times over the years I made that same maneuver going into the living room. We were sitting in Stan's living room talking. I told him how I had missed the Delmar bus to go downtown to submit an application for a job at the Mart Building.

Stan's position regarding submitting a job application after nine o'clock in the morning was the same as mine. Stan said, "Lumps, I think you did the right thing." So we determined that going the next day to submit the application was better than showing up after nine o'clock. With that being said, Stan and I just hung out, chilling and shooting the breeze about everything and nothing. As usual we talked about girls. That was always part of our conversations; at 18 or 19 years old, girls were predominantly on our minds. We were talking about some truths, exaggerating, talking smack, or just plain outright telling lies. It was part of the fun we shared. At the time, I didn't have a steady girlfriend, or any girlfriend. At the time I don't think Stan had a girlfriend that he was serious about.

I had been at Stan's house for about two hours when I decided to go home. It seemed that every time I put my foot on the next step to leave the porch, Stan would comment about something to start another conversation.

I think he was intent on delaying me as long as he could, basically with idle conversation. So we would start shooting the breeze all over again, about nothing in particular. While still standing on his front porch and talking, I repeatedly said, "Stan, man, I am leaving now." We were on the front porch for 30 minutes. There must have been a reason why Stan continually delayed me from leaving his house and why I so willingly cooperated.

CHAPTER 12

———— ◇ ————

A Ride with Tim Taylor

———— ◇ ————

I WAS FINALLY READY TO leave Stan's house when a friend named Tim Taylor, whom Stan and I both knew very well, was driving up the street in front of Stan's house. Tim beeped his horn and we both waved and hollered as he drove past the house. Tim beeped his horn again, acknowledging us and continued to drive up the street. Seeing Tim sparked another conversation, so we continued talking. Less than ten minutes later, Tim came driving back down the street going east. Stan yelled out Tim's name to flag him down. There were no cars behind him, so he stopped in the middle of the street. When I rushed down off the porch toward Tim's car, he rolled down the window, smiling, and said, "Hey, Willis, you are pretty far from home. I guess you had to check on Stan, to keep him straight." He then started to laugh.

As I was approaching Tim's car, I asked if he was going near Taylor and Enright, where I lived. Tim said, "Yes, I am going that way. Come on, Willis, get in. You know you can ride down with me anytime."

I got in the car. Naturally, we started catching up on how each of us was doing and what was going on in our lives. I told Tim that I had struggled during my first year in college and I was recollecting myself to focus on my future. We continued to talk mostly man talk, asking about mutual friends and acquaintances, who was doing what, etc. I don't know how the subject came up, but I told Tim that I was supposed to go downtown that morning to the Mart Building to put in a job application. But, because *I missed the bus*, I would have arrived after nine o'clock, so I decided I would go tomorrow.

Taking his eyes off the road for a few seconds and looking directly at me, Tim said, "Willis, this is ironic. I am actually on my way to the St. Louis City Police Academy across the street from the Mart Building. Man, I'm going right down there to Twelfth and Spruce Streets. Believe me! It's not too late. It is not quite noon yet. Come on man, ride downtown with me. It's not too late for you to put in the job application."

Tim was three or four years older than me, but our paths crossed sociably now and then. Vocationally, Tim was a licensed professional barber, and worked in his father's barbershop. The barber shop was named Friendly's Barbershop, located on Taylor and Enright Avenues just around the corner from where I lived. Tim had a strong clientele among most of the younger customers who came to the barbershop.

I saw Tim frequently since I usually got my hair cut every two weeks. We would have normal down-to-earth conversations all the time in the barbershop. Tim also graduated from Sumner High School three or four years before I did. Tim's brother David Taylor graduated with me in the class of June 1958. Tim's father, Reverend Taylor, was the pastor at his own church. I know Tim was a Christian and was raised in the church.

As convinced as I had been earlier that morning that it was too late for me to put in a job application, after talking with Tim, I was now just as certain that it wasn't too late to put in my job application, even though it was close to noon! So I rode downtown with Tim, and he dropped me off at the Mart Building, on the corner of Twelfth and Spruce Streets. Waiting for the traffic light to turn green, the thought of the time raced through my mind repeatedly! But I didn't have any real doubt about putting in the application at this time. All I could hope for was that putting in my job application would go well for me. When the traffic light turned green, I walked with confidence into the Mart Building.

I entered the lobby of the Mart Building. This was a government building, I asked at the information desk for directions to the Daily Record Company's personnel office. I was directed to the elevators located in the lobby and told to ask the elevator operator to take me to the Daily Records Company. Their personnel office was located on the eighth floor. They also had office space on both the seventh and eighth floors where their three hundred–plus employees worked.

I remember getting off the elevator, and there were several rows of desks positioned throughout the office work areas. Some people were sitting at their desk eating their lunch and reading the newspaper. There were a few people still working at their desks as well.

I walked down the aisle to the personnel office. There were two offices in that wing directly across from each other. One office was the project manager's office, which was on the left and the personnel office was on the right.

It took me about thirty seconds to walk to the personnel office. Although it was a very short walk, it seemed like an eternity to me. I couldn't relax since I didn't know what to expect. Subconsciously I was anticipating an unfavorable reception because it was well past the normal time to put in a job application.

When I finally reached the personnel office, there was only one person in the office. I assumed that the other people who worked in the office were out to lunch. I was still a little hesitant about asking for a job application at that late hour.

The office door was wide open but I paused at the threshold instead of just walking into the office. I just waited, as if there were lead weights on my feet. There was a man sitting at his desk, his head was down reading the newspaper while eating his lunch. He was holding the newspaper with both hands, almost covering his entire face. Apparently, he did not realize I was standing in the doorway.

I was hesitant to disturb him while he was eating his lunch and reading the newspaper. I just continued standing silently in the doorway for what felt like several minutes. I still had not crossed the threshold to enter the office.

All of a sudden, the man's head jerked straight up as if he had been startled, not like he was frightened, but more like he was bewildered or alarmed. In a concerned tone, he asked, "Can I help you?" It was a question, but it seemed more like a demand.

I was still somewhat concerned about asking for a job application at noon. I answered the man, smiling as I said with a pleasant tone, "Yes sir, good afternoon. I would like to put in an application for a job."

He immediately got up from his chair. When he stood up, I realized he was about six feet tall and had a slender build. He appeared to be in his late forties. He had gray hair and a neatly trimmed gray mustache. He was neatly dressed, and his clothes fit him well. He didn't say another word. He walked to the desk to the right and got a job application. He gave me the application and motioned for me to sit at a table and fill out the application. Later I learned that the desk where the applications were kept was the personnel secretary's desk.

He returned to his desk and resumed reading his newspaper and eating his lunch. He didn't give me any instructions about completing the application and he didn't say another word to me while I was completing the application. The job application was basically straightforward and routine. I provided my personal information, name, address, age, and ethnicity; I don't recall any questions pertaining to any job experience I had.

I completed the application in about twenty minutes. I gave the completed application to the man and thanked him as I left the office. At that point, the other four people who worked in the personnel office had not returned from their thirty-minute lunch break.

Technically, I never went through a formal interview for the job. This was my first job application experience for a "real" job. However, I recall feeling encouraged after I had completed the application. I don't know particularly why I had that feeling. I found out later, after I was hired for the job, that the man's name was Arthur McGuire and everybody called him Art.

CHAPTER 13

◇

Working for the Daily Record Company

◇

I N APRIL 1959, I FILLED out an application for a job at the Daily Record Company (DRC). I was hired by Mr. Arthur (Art) McGuire and started working on May 4, 1959. At that time, I wasn't sure about my job responsibilities, but it didn't matter; I was grateful to have a job.

I vaguely recall riding the Delmar bus that morning with my sister Shirley, to get downtown to the Mart Building. We rode the bus downtown to Twelfth Street. We then caught the Twelfth Street bus and rode to Spruce Street. We arrived at the Mart Building at 7:40 a.m. Shirley was a friendly person and was greeted by several people in the lobby of the building.

Shirley introduced me to Lee, the elevator operator and told him it was my first day on the job. Lee was an African-American man in his early forties, and he was very friendly. We shook hands, and he wished me good luck on the job. He said I would be fine if I was like my sister because she was sharp. We laughed and I thanked him. Shirley walked with me to the personnel office; like I needed help. That was the big sister in her.

Ruth Rolfing, the secretary, was the only person in the personnel office when I arrived that morning. I still remember Ruth smiling when I identified myself. She told me that Art McGuire, the personnel administrator, would be arriving shortly to talk to me about the job. Ruth asked me to sit in the chair where the typewriter was located.

At eight o'clock Gene Bowyer and a young guy named Michael came in the office. Michael sat in a chair next to Gene Bowyer's desk. Then Paul Drake came in the office. Art McGuire came into the office a few minutes later.

He smiled and shook my hand as he said, "Welcome on board, Willis."

He then introduced me to everyone in the office. He said Gene Bowyer was the annual leave and sick leave accountant. Michael was the messenger, and I would be replacing him. Paul Drake was the payroll accountant who computed the employees' weekly payroll. Paul was a large white man about six feet two or three inches tall and in his mid to late thirties.

Art explained that I would be part of the personnel team, and he knew everyone would help me get adjusted to the job. I was the only African-American in the personnel office. Art explained that I was hired to replace Michael, the messenger, who was going into the military. As he looked at him, he said in a joking way, "I tried to talk good sense into Michael."

Initially, Art joked around with Michael about joining the service, but he became more serious and told him it was an honorable thing to serve in the military and that he would be home in two years before he knew it.

Art formally introduced me to Michael and asked him to show me what I had to do on the job. That was the first time I was informed of the job description and the responsibilities. Of course, it didn't make any difference to me. The fact was I now had a regular job.

Michael was 19 or 20 years old, just a little older than me. He was tall, slender, and pleasant. I could tell immediately that he was a nice guy.

I was excited about starting to work, and I appreciated the opportunity to get firsthand job training from Michael. He told me that we would make our first mail pickup at nine o'clock.

On our first mail pickup, we walked through the typing pool area where my sister Shirley worked. When I saw her, I started grinning from ear to ear, waved, and said hello to her. She waved back to me with a sense of pride and a smile on her face. I told Michael that the lady I spoke to was my sister. He said that he knew Shirley and she was really nice. They spoke to each other all the time.

We continued making the rounds of picking up the mail, and Michael explained everything I needed to know. Learning my job was very easy. Basically, I just had to remember the mail stops. Michael introduced me to the secretaries in the four divisions where I had to pick up and drop off mail. It was obvious that Michael was well liked by the division secretaries. In fact, just about everyone he encountered seemed to like him.

Michael told me that his mother was a Federal Civil Service employee in the Mart Building on the fifth floor. So we went down to the fifth floor and he introduced me to his mom. She was a nice lady, and she welcomed me to the job and wished me well. Although Michael's brother also worked at the Mart Building as a Federal Civil Service employee on the fourth floor, I did not get a chance to meet him that day.

There were just a few African-Americans who held Federal Civil Service office jobs at the Mart Building; I recall two African-American men who worked in the office area on the fifth floor. One was Mr. Cason. He was a light-brown skinned man, very professional looking and in his early fifties. He always wore a bowtie and a suit to work. If someone wanted a role model in professionalism, he was the man. The other African-American man was Mr. Gibson. I remember that he was also very professional, but he didn't dress as formally as Mr. Cason. Mr. Gibson also trained boxers in the Golden Gloves. His son Dewey also boxed. There were several other Federal Civil Service African-American men who worked in the mailroom and the GSA supply room office and several African-American women who worked as Federal Civil Service employees.

Michael had only one week to train me on everything that I needed to know about the job. He was expected to report to the Army for basic training the following week. I became very familiar with the routine for the mail pickup and drop-off locations. I also established a friendly rapport with all of the division secretaries and most of the people I encountered on the job.

The job was basically rudimentary. By Thursday of that week, I asked Michael to let me do the mail pickup and drop-offs by myself. I explained that I would be more confident in performing the job next week if I had an opportunity to do it independently while he was still there to answer questions.

Not only did I learn the routine for the job very well, but I was also able to establish a professional and friendly relationship with everyone in the personnel office. The work environment was excellent. I didn't have any problems on Thursday or Friday with the mail pickup and drop-off deliveries that I made without Michael. The job functions were repetitive.

On Friday, Michael's last day of work, there was a small farewell party for him in the personnel office. Several people from the four divisions, including the secretaries, came to wish him farewell. His mother and brother attended, and the young ladies from the typing pool also stopped by, including my sister Shirley.

I personally thanked Michael for showing me how to do the job. I told him that he had truly trained me well. We both laughed as he said, "Willis, you knew what to do after the first day that I showed you the routine. Training you was easy."

As we made the final mail rounds together that day, Michael explained that he was going into the military because he believed he would have a better chance of getting a Federal Civil Service job after serving in the military.

There were probably three hundred plus employees working for DRC and very few were African-American. Most of the African-Americans were women; they either worked in the typing pool or were clerks in the technical file area. There may have been eight African-American men who were catalogers or technical equipment technicians.

I know that I was blessed. I had my first job as an adult and I was working in an office. I was earning a living for myself. The job required a certain dress code; I wore a shirt and necktie to work with a neat pair of pants and sport coat. A professional look was always required.

Working in an office environment did have some advantages. Right or wrong, as an African- American wearing a necktie and sport coat, I got a more positive reaction from people riding the bus than an individual dressed as a laborer. Also, because I worked at the Mart Building, it was perceived that I had a good job. When I wanted to do business with a bank, working at the Mart Building had weight on the loan application.

I felt fortunate to work in the personnel office under Art McGuire's supervision. He was the personnel administrator responsible for filling the job openings in the company. When I started working for the DRC, I was 18 years old. I was now in what I considered my era as the messenger for the DRC. My job responsibilities were primarily to make four mail pickups a day.

I was also responsible for getting coffee and lunch from the cafeteria for the personnel staff. I made a coffee pickup in the morning and at two o'clock in the afternoon. Periodically I had to go to the post office to purchase postage stamps. I am sure my job as messenger was the lowest classification and the lowest-paying job in the company. My starting salary was one dollar per hour.

Ruth Rolfing's Help and Influence

I met Ruth Rolfing on Monday, May 4, the first day I reported to work. She was sitting at her desk as if it had been orchestrated for her to be there when I arrived. In several ways I was entering into a different phase of my life. This was my first job as an adult young man having to support myself at 18 years old. I wasn't sure what to expect from the people I would be working with, but it was uplifting to be greeted by Ruth that first day on the job. She had a pleasant smile and I immediately felt comfortable that everything was going to be just fine for me. I was impressed by the way Ruth had welcomed me; it set the stage for the remainder of my employment at the DRC.

I am not sure why, but Ruth reminded me of my mother. Possibly because she had a beautiful smile and a positive personality like my mother. Also, she took me under her wings immediately. From the beginning, Ruth told me that if I had any problems on the job to let her know and she would make sure Art would address them. Ruth's actions were parental-like, as she helped to navigate me through the office work environment of this predominantly white male workforce. When Ruth would make subtle or direct suggestions about certain individuals or situations; I always took her advice.

I didn't have a desk; I had a chair next to Gene Bowyer's desk. Gene was an exceptionally nice guy, very reserved and soft spoken. He was 27 or 28 years old, about five feet, eight inches tall and weighed approximately 160 pounds. His hair was always neatly cut. He was married with two children. His daughter was five years old, and his son was three years old. Normally we talked about common things of interest but not about politics or race issues.

This was 1959 in St. Louis and there were plenty of race issues in the newspapers and on television daily. However, in the personnel office, those subjects were not a topic of discussion. Working in such a small physical work space and having controversial discussions that could turn out to be heated could have resulted in an uncomfortable work environment for everyone.

Fortunately, my work routine allowed me to watch Gene Bowyer do his job. He answered any questions I had about his job, and he explained the functions of his job in detail. As a result, I was able to actually learn Gene's job.

Every day, Gene continued to show me detailed information about his job. I was able to spend time learning Gene's job because I could do my messenger's job in three hours during the entire day. I think it actually only took me two weeks to completely learn Gene's job.

In Sumner High School. I took three years of machine operations on the lathe and other equipment and mechanical drawing in lieu of a typing course. I knew how to create mechanical drawings and read blueprints and schematic drawings, which was very beneficial to me during my work career. To occupy time between my mail pickups, I also asked Ruth's permission to practice typing on the typewriter in the personnel office.

Ruth gave me tips on how to type better and faster. Eventually I became competent with my typing skills. Ruth would give me typing exercises to practice. After a month of practice, she timed me; I was able to type about 30 words a minute.

Art McGuire's Influence

One morning after I had been on the job for three weeks, I was going to the cafeteria to get coffee for the morning coffee break. Virginia, the secretary in the Surface and Marine Department, asked me to bring her supervisor a cup of coffee. Virginia's office was next to the personnel office. I told her I would and when I returned to give Virginia the coffee, Art appeared. He was somewhat agitated and told Virginia in a loud voice that I was not a "gopher" to get coffee for her supervisor. He told her that she should get her supervisor's coffee and not ask me to do that again. Apparently, Ruth or Art heard Virginia ask me to bring her supervisor a cup of coffee.

Virginia was embarrassed and I was caught off guard by Art's strong reaction to that situation. Virginia was a year older than me and she was a friendly person. We talked casually every day. She was cool! However, Art saw the need to nip it in the bud so that neither Virginia nor anyone else would ask me to get coffee or run errands. I was independent enough that I was not going to let someone take unfair advantage of me. I was always taught by my parents to speak up for myself; I was not bashful about defending myself. I appreciated that Art did not consider me a runner or gopher for people in the company.

I believe the position that Art took about me getting coffee for Virginia and his verbal public denunciation let it be known that I was valued as an employee of the company even if I was "just a messenger." It did not take long for the word to spread that I was highly thought of by the people in the personnel office.

Art was responsible for deciding how and when to address my concerns or requests. I don't recall one time that I asked for anything that it didn't come out the way I was hoping it would. At the time, I didn't know his story about what happened when I applied for the job. Two years later Art told me that a voice said just two words to him, *"Hire him."* In writing this book, I have thought about the promotions and advantages I received while working for the DRC. Perhaps Art was still being influenced by the initial voice he heard when I applied for the job. Given the social, political, and economic climate during that time, it wasn't easy for African-Americans to get a fair shake in the job market. I have to believe that the Holy Spirit extended His long arms over a far and wide area on my behalf.

However, that doesn't mean that I didn't witness some form of discriminatory practices when African-Americans came to apply for a job. That old adage was apparently true; *it wasn't what you know as much as who you know that got you hired.* In this case, metaphorically speaking,I had been the recipient of nepotism at the supreme highest, the Holy Spirit. That is how I was hired.

During this time (1959 and 1960), there was an African-American female employee named Ina Boon who worked in the typing pool at DRC. She was a strong advocate for fair and equal hiring practices at the DRC. I don't know if Ina's threats to have the National Association for the Advancement of Colored People (NAACP) investigate the hiring practices of the DRC precipitated the hiring of more African-Americans, but eventually more African-Americans were hired.

My sister Shirley would often tell me how much Ina respected me as a young African-American man. Ina was a tall, slender brown-skinned woman with large eyes. She would speak her mind and didn't care who heard her when she was speaking about something that wasn't right. Ina would often complain to the unit chief in the typing pool about the lack of promotions of young African-American women who had experience and tenure with the company. Ironically, Ina Boon later became an influencing force with the NAACP.

Gene Bowyer's Vacation

Gene Bowyer planned to take a two-week vacation. Since there was no staff backup for Gene's position, the company hired a temporary employee to cover the period that he would be out of the office. They hired a man named Russ, who knew the project manager, Mr. Hamilton. He appeared to be a man in his mid-thirties, with a medium-build, somewhat athletic-looking, about five feet eight inches tall. He had a full head of light brown hair. I found Russ to have a pleasing personality. He was a likable person, very cordial, with a friendly sense of humor.

Gene trained Russ for one week before he went on vacation. During the day, I could hear Gene explaining his job to Russ. Russ would ask questions and Gene replied with detailed information.

On Monday morning, as usual, I started with my daily rounds of picking up the mail, getting coffee, and dropping off mail to the individual department secretaries. Russ was in the office sitting at Gene's desk and Art McGuire, Ruth Rolfing, and Paul Drake were at their desks. Russ had pulled out the annual and sick leave cards that he had to update for the past pay period. The file was in alphabetical order, and Gene had showed Russ how to process the cards in sequential order so that all of the employee leave records could be updated.

After I returned from my first mail run, Russ still had the leave cards with the names starting with A in front of him. Russ was being hesitant in calculating the totals to write on the leave cards. He had added several totals on the adding machine, but he had not written information on the cards. He was struggling.

I was sitting in the chair next to Russ and trying to be inconspicuous as I watched him repeatedly shuffle the same annual and sick leave cards on his desk. Russ was getting flushed in his face and beginning to sweat a little. I could tell that he was puzzled about what he was supposed to do. Obviously, I didn't know Russ as well as I knew Gene Bowyer. I didn't know if he would accept my suggestions or resent me asking if he needed help. I decided to ask him if he had a problem with anything or if he needed help.

Russ explained that he thought he had everything down pat before Gene left but he could not recall how to balance the leave records. He knew he was missing a step somewhere in the process and he was baffled.

I told Russ that I had watched Gene handle the leave card and that I might be able to tell him what step he was missing. Russ and I changed chairs, and I sat at the desk. I started working the A alphabetical list of the leave record cards and showed Russ what he had missed or had done wrong. When Mr. Hamilton walked into the office, Russ told him that I knew how to do this job. He said, "SW (Mr. Hamilton's name), did you know that Willis knows how to do Gene's job? He showed me what I didn't remember about the process that Gene taught me."

Mr. Hamilton was smiling and said that it didn't surprise him at all. He claimed that I probably could learn his job too. Ruth Rolfing pitched in with a comment, "I bet you that we all will end up working for Willis one day." Everyone nodded their heads and laughed. After I had showed Russ what to do, he was able to hold down Gene's job until Gene returned from vacation.

CHAPTER 14

$\diamond$

Promoted from My Messenger's Job

$\diamond$

I HAD BEEN WORKING FOR the Daily Record Company for about two and a half months and I really liked my job. Granted, I was only a messenger, but this was 1959 in St. Louis, MO, and office jobs weren't very accessible to African-Americans. I knew there weren't many African-American teenagers who worked in a white-collar office environment.

Working in the personnel office, I had a positive networking connection with Ruth Rolfing. I could talk to her very candidly. I came to work early one morning and Ruth was in early also, so I asked if she had a few minutes to talk. I told her I really like working in the personnel office but I thought I had learned all that I could in the messenger's job.

I said, "I would like to get a job where I can learn more technical work. I don't know exactly how I should go about trying to get a promotion to another job." Ruth said, "Willis, let me talk to Art and see what he thinks."

Less than two weeks later, Art told me that he and Mr. Hamilton had agreed to promote me to a file clerk job down on the seventh floor. I would be working for Ms. Elsie Baker, the supervisor in the technical file retrieval area. He said the position was also a pay raise for me.

However, Art said I was responsible for getting my replacement for the messenger job. I was also told that if my replacement did not work out, I would return to my old job. Mr. Hamilton's ultimatum put a lot of pressure as to who I should recommend as my replacement. Stanley McKissic, my very best friend, was my first choice.

However, I knew Stan did not have the temperament for the messenger job. It would have been hard for me not to recommend Stan for the job if he wanted it. When I explained exactly what was involved in the messenger job, I was relieved that Stan agreed he was not really suited for the messenger job. He already had a job, even though it was not an office job. So I thought about another friend, Cleart Jones. Stan agreed that Cleart would be a good fit for the messenger job.

Everyone in our neighborhood said Cleart was such a nice dude and mild mannered and quiet. At the time Cleart was working in the local poolroom. Stan and I met Cleart at Yea's, a Chinese restaurant that we frequented.

At the restaurant Stan and I sat on the same side in the booth and Cleart sat across from us. The three of us discussed the job. I told Cleart that I had gotten a promotion and my messenger job was now available. I explained that I could choose my replacement and that Stan already had a job. Stan interrupted me and said, "Cleart, you know me. If one of those white dudes said something I didn't like, it would be me and him." We laughed. Cleart replied, "You know that's right, Stan." I told him that if he wanted the job, I would recommend him. Before I could get the words out of my mouth, he said emphatically, "Yes, Willis, I want the job." We all laughed.

I explained to Cleart that if he did not work out on the job, the project manager would bring me back, so I wanted to explain the job duties to him very clearly. I told Cleart that the title of the job was messenger and that he would be responsible for picking up and delivering the internal mail within the four departments. He would get coffee for the personnel staff during the morning and afternoon breaks and go to the cafeteria to get their lunch. The mail pickups were at 9:00 a.m., 11:30 a.m., and between 3:00 and 3:30 p.m.

I let him know that the job paid one dollar an hour, and he would get paid every two weeks. He would get a two-week vacation and one week of sick leave time accrued during the year. He was required to wear casual dress clothes and be neatly dressed. However, I often wore a tie to work. I told him that the people in the personnel office were terrific to work with and that the job wasn't difficult. I would train him well. I told him that I knew he was going to work out just fine.

I told Cleart to be ready Monday morning at seven to catch the Delmar bus with me and my sister Shirley. That Monday morning Cleart was standing on the corner waiting for us. He was neatly dressed and smiling as always. He said he was excited about getting the job. Shirley told him that she knew he would do well in the job. She said, "Just be yourself and listen to what Willis tells you."

After we arrived at the Mart Building, Cleart and I went to the personnel office and I introduced him to Ruth. Ruth gave him some paperwork to complete. While he was filling out the papers, Art McGuire came into the office and I introduced him as well.

As they shook hands, Art said, "Just call me Art. If you are a friend of Willis I know you will do a good job. Willis knows what our agreement is, so I know he made a good choice in selecting you as his replacement."

I introduced Cleart to Gene Bowyer, Paul Drake, Mr. Hamilton, the project manager, and Joyce Morrow, who was Mr. Hamilton's secretary.

Before we left for the first mail pickup, Mr. Hamilton noticed Cleart sitting in the chair next to Gene Bowyer's desk with a toothpick in his mouth. Mr. Hamilton stood in the office for a minute and then asked if he could speak to me.

We went into his secretary's office and he said, "Willis, it doesn't look professional for Cleart to have a toothpick in his mouth sitting here in the office. Please let him know that he shouldn't do that." I told Mr. Hamilton that I would let Cleart know and that I was sure it was just an oversight on his part and it wouldn't happen again.

When I told Cleart what Mr. Hamilton had said about the toothpick, he was embarrassed. He took the toothpick from his mouth and promised it would not happen again. I understood that during the late 1950s and the 1960s, it was popular for some young African-American males to keep a toothpick in their mouths all the time. It was a style thing and Cleart was one of many young males from our neighborhood who kept a toothpick in his mouth.

That first day, I started his training. I explained exactly what he needed to know, and how and when to do it. I introduced Cleart to all the people he would come into contact with. Among the young department secretaries, I was considered to be a pretty cool dude and a very likable guy. The division chiefs seemed to like me as well, although it probably wasn't totally genuine. I felt confident that over time Cleart would also establish a good relationship with the employees.

When Cleart and I went to the cafeteria on that first day, I also introduced him to the cafeteria workers on the food-serving line. I let them know that he would be replacing me because I had a new job and I would be working on the seventh floor.

Mr. Hamilton's comment about the toothpick in his mouth was the only unfavorable comment about Cleart as the messenger. Ultimately, Cleart had a very successful job as a messenger with the Daily Record Company, as well as a substantial and successful Federal Civil Service career. He retired with twenty-plus years of service that started with the messenger job in 1959.

◇

CHAPTER 15

Working in the Technical File Retrieval Area

◇

I HAD TRAINED CLEART FOR a week so he would know the ins and outs of the messenger job as well as I did. I was now embarking on a new job adventure. I don't know if it was strategic of Art McGuire or just coincidental, but I was going to be the first or second male file clerk to work in the technical file retrieval area (TFRA).

That morning Art walked with me to the TFRA work area and told me to work as I always did and everything would be fine. The technical workers on the seventh and eighth floors were classified as supply catalogers and equipment specialists. They wrote the technical descriptions for the replacement parts and items that appeared in the army's technical manuals (TMs).

The TFRA work area was encased by file cabinets positioned in a U shape up against the back wall. The workers entered the area from the front open area. The supply catalogers and equipment specialists would wait outside of the work area when they requested a technical file jacket. Since the file cabinets were waist high, the catalogers and equipment specialists used them to write the file jacket request.

Standing outside of the work area, Art asked the supervisor, Ms. Elsie Baker, to come over to the file cabinets and he introduced me. He told Elsie that she was getting an excellent worker. As he was leaving, Art told me to stop by the office sometime to let everyone know how things were going. I believe Art's comment was for Elsie's benefit as much as it was for mine. I think he wanted her to know that I had people in the personnel office who were watching out for me.

Since I was working on the seventh floor, I wouldn't see Art, Ruth, and the other people in the personnel office regularly. However, I stayed in contact with all of them; every now and then I would stop by the personnel office and say hello to everyone.

The same day that I started working as a file clerk, a young white 19 year-old male named Elijah also started to work in TFRA. Elijah was sitting at a table where we would eventually share a work space, and we were trained together.

Elijah was one of the nicest guys I met on the job. He was a rural kid from a farm in southeast Missouri. He was about six feet tall, average size and weight for his height, wore eyeglasses and had thick black hair. He had an odd walk; he would bob up and down from his waist with every step he made, like what would be considered a country walk. I really liked Elijah and we had fun working together.

It was interesting to note that Elijah and I changed the all-female workgroup in the file clerk area to a coed environment. The file clerk work area had about fifteen women, five or six of which were African-American and appeared to be older and more mature than their white counterparts.

Elsie Baker, the supervisor, was in her early fifties, and very knowledgeable about the TFRA. A younger woman named Helen was Elsie's assistant; she was in charge when Elsie was out of the file area. She was 23 or 24 years old.

After several months of working in the TFRA, I noticed there were individual cliques among the women. On any particular day there would be three or four women, both white and African- American, upset with another group of women who were also white and African- American. I didn't know if the problems were just catty women issues, vindictive behavior, or a tit-for-tat situation. This behavior seemed to permeate throughout the TFRA work area and continued week after week. Elijah and I were able to stay clear of becoming directly involved in these issues. Having Elijah as a coworker helped me to maintain my balance working in the TFRA.

After five or six months, I had learned most of the information from reading the technical documents in the file jackets. I was familiar with federal stock numbers, manufacturer's part numbers, reference numbers, item names, nomenclatures, and end item applications. I talked to the supply catalogers so I could understand how they wrote an item description. I understood the process of how the technical descriptive information on a manuscript plate would be photographed. I learned that the illustrators would use the photographed pages to publish the army's technical manual (TM).

One day I reached my tipping point with the bickering. I was uncomfortable. I felt that I had to get out of the TFRA work area. I went to see Ruth Rolfing and explained my dilemma. I told her that I was very unhappy working in the TFRA because of the bickering and did not enjoy coming to work anymore. Also, I had learned all that I could from that job.

Ruth understood and said that she would talk with Art and get back to me. As I was leaving the office, I said hello to Gene Bowyer. Gene said hello in his normal, jovial way and asked me how I was doing. I told him that I was hanging in there. He said to tell Mary that he said hello. I had been working for the Daily Record Company for three months when I first met Mary and I had mentioned her to Gene and Ruth from time to time. I smiled and said, "Thanks. I will tell her." Gene would playfully tease me; he said that he could tell from the way I talked about Mary that I was serious about her.

Art McGuire Creates a Job for Me

Less than two weeks after I talked to Ruth, Elsie called me over to her desk and told me to go see Art McGuire in the personnel office. When I walked into the personnel office, Art greeted me and I spoke to everyone in the office. He said, "Willis, pull up a chair and sit down." Art explained that he had created a job for me. I would be the supply stock clerk for the Daily Record Company. Instead of the department secretaries ordering supplies from the GSA Supply Office weekly, I would request the supplies from the GSA Supply Office on a monthly basis. Then I would issue supplies to the secretaries on a weekly basis when they submitted their requisitions.

Art said, "Willis, come on with me." He walked with Cleart and me to the warehouse area. Outside of the fire door, there was an empty storage room. The storeroom was a large vacant area with storage shelves along the wall inside the door. Art gave me the key to the door and told me that there was a lot of space in this storeroom and I should clean it up and arrange it the way I wanted. He said he would order a desk for me and it should be delivered later in the day.

This job was a blessed opportunity for me. It was more than my talk with Ruth, her talk with Art McGuire, and his creation of a new position for me. It seemed that every time I asked for an opportunity, it was made available for me. I believe getting this job was also spiritually influenced! I didn't realize at the time that Art was the individual who was being used as my guardian angel. I didn't learn this fact until about eight months later, when Art told me about the spiritual experience that he had when I first applied for the job.

I was given approval from Art McGuire to set up the supply storeroom as I determined. I organized the room so that it was a professional business office. During the workday, Cleart and I stayed in the supply storeroom. It was cool to have my own office where Cleart and I could shoot the breeze and enjoy the workday. Between his messenger runs, Cleart would be in the supply storeroom with me. Both of us knew all the young people who worked at the company. Some of them would stop by our office on their morning or afternoon breaks and during the day just to get away from their normal work area. We were cautious about young female employees, particularly the young white girls, coming into the office, so we always kept the office door open when there were females in our office.

I was well liked and respected by the people throughout the Mart Building, especially the employees of the Daily Record Company. The African-American employees thought I was a cool brother and I also established friendships with many of the young white male and female employees in the company. There were several guys with whom I had a meaningful relationship; and occasionally I played baseball with them.

When I submitted the monthly supply request with the GSA supply office, two workers from the first floor would deliver the supplies. They were friendly mature African-American men in their thirties and would tease Cleart and me, calling us "young bloods." Cleart and I would then restock the shelves in the stockroom. We had a substantial inventory on hand for commonly ordered supplies.

Supply Office Decision

I had been the supply stock clerk for six or seven months when Art McGuire told me that the GSA Office said my job was a duplication of the GSA function. The Daily Record Company shouldn't have a position for stocking and issuing their own office supplies, when managing, stocking, and issuing office supplies was a function of the GSA Office. I don't know what prompted the GSA Office to eliminate my position; perhaps my job as a supply stock clerk was a threat to the GSA workers.

CHAPTER 16

◇

Mother's Vision Foreseeing
Mary as My Wife

◇

The Meeting—Mary Ann Byas and Willis Drake

A S I WROTE EARLIER, IF my mother had the same vision three times, that was confirmation that the vision would happen just as the Holy Spirit had revealed it to her.

In 1956 I was a 16 year old sophomore at Sumner High School, when my mother told me that she had a vision three times of a light-brown-skinned girl—she was a very pretty girl—who would be my wife. Mother then said, "Willis, you watch yourself."

Three years later, in 1959, I had recovered from my college withdrawal and everything was going well with my life. I was doing well on my job. I had my own money and I did not need any financial help from my parents. I paid a modest amount for room and board at home. My social life was cool. I was hanging out with my friends and having fun. My best friend, Stan, and I agreed to participate in the Golden Gloves for one more year.

The earliest that Stan and I would go to Tandy Gym was mid-October; going to Tandy Gym before October was not customary for veteran boxers like us. We would report after the novice boxers had reported for training in September and were not reprimanded by the boxing coach.

I don't recall exactly why I decided to go to Tandy Gym that particular day; going to the gym early in September was an anomaly. For me to go to the gym that early before the boxing season started, had to be both a spontaneous and impromptu decision. I do not know if it was a spiritual intuition or what it was. Maybe it was a power greater than me that somehow directed me to go to Tandy Gym that evening.

The route that Stan and I walked to the gym that evening dictated that we would walk past the Billy Burkes' Restaurant located in the 1900 block of Pendleton; usually we walked across Newstead or Taylor Avenue to get to Tandy Gym. Whatever the reason that we walked across Pendleton Avenue that day is beyond my understanding.

Unbeknown to me, my future fate and my mother's vision would be fulfilled due to the events happening that evening. There are too many variables that took place that allowed us to meet that day; therefore, it is impossible for me to subscribe to the possibility that Mary and I met by chance. I believe the events leading up to meeting Mary Ann Byas that evening were beyond my human control. Undeniably, there was a spiritual presence that inspired me to go to the gym that day, at that time, taking the route I did, for a reason; but I did not experience a spiritual message in the way that the Holy Spirit had spoken to Art McGuire in 1959 on my behalf.

Billy Burkes' Restaurant was located a few blocks from Homer G. Philips Nursing School, Sumner High School, and the Tandy Center (gym). Most of the students patronized Billy Burkes' because of their delicious hamburgers.

I am sure that we would not have stopped in Billy Burkes' that evening. At the precise moment that Stan and I walked by Billy Burkes', three young ladies walked out, practically bumping into us, making that moment more special. What's the possibility that at that exact moment, Mary and I would enter into the same physical space?

Naturally, seeing those gorgeous young ladies immediately changed our focus. Getting to Tandy Gym was no longer a priority; so I believe I was meant to meet Mary at that specific moment,

Stan and I were two confident young men, and we both had a swagger about us. We were fairly good-looking guys, had jobs, dressed well, and considered ourselves to be cool and intelligent. Therefore, seeing these three fine sisters automatically turned our heads.

I don't believe our meeting was a serendipitous encounter; I could surmise that the stars were in alignment, a guardian angel was sitting on each of our shoulders, or it was a spiritual connection that was supposed to happen. My conjecture is that Mary and I were supposed to meet when we did.

As I think back on that evening, I know it was my destiny. I was blessed that day! That is the only plausible explanation for what happened, chemistry-wise, between Mary and me when we first met.

Within a day after meeting this fine young lady, Mary Ann Byas, I was totally smitten by her and Mary was mutually captivated by me as well. Only once had Mother's vision of the girl I would marry cross my mind. Those thoughts of the vision had rarely entered my consciousness over the past three years; throughout high school, I just went about trying to meet girls as a normal teenager does.

It still warms my heart and I smile when I think about the events that led to our meeting. It was early September 1959 and a very nice day. Mary had enrolled at the Homer G. Phillips Nursing School only a few weeks earlier.

Stan and I had worked that day, so it wasn't as if we needed something to occupy our time or burn off energy by walking to the gym. We were not bored young men; we had an active work and social life. I was optimistic about how things were going for me overall. I was not looking for any fill-in time because I did not have something meaningful to do.

Now the human-interest story begins. It did not take any persuasion between Stan and me to divert our attention from going to our planned destination, Tandy Gym; we immediately switched our thoughts to these young ladies.

The five of us were standing in front of Billy Burkes'. Fortunately I happened to know Constance Fitzpatrick, who we called Connie. I had not seen her in a year, so we said hello and Connie started talking to me with a big smile on her face, almost laughing. She said, "Willis, I brought my two friends to Billy Burkes' to taste the best hamburgers in the world."

111

All of us laughed and I asked Connie's friends if they were disappointed. They both said, "No, we were not disappointed. Those hamburgers were really good." Stan and I both agreed because we had eaten a lot of hamburgers at Billy Burkes'.

I knew Connie from the Tandy Center dances when we were in high school. Connie was a student at Beaumont High School, which at that time had more white students than African-American students.

I asked Connie to introduce us to her friends. She said, "Willis, we are classmates attending Homer G. Philips's Nursing School." Pointing to Grace, she said, "This is Grace." Then touching Mary on her left shoulder, who was standing next to her, Connie said, "And this is Mary." She then said, "Grace and Mary, this is Willis." Looking at Stan, Connie said, "I do not know your name." I said, "Connie, that is my friend Stanley McKissic. He and I are always together. You must remember him." She looked at Stan for a few seconds and said, "Yes, maybe I have seen him at Tandy before."

Tandy Community Center

Connie said, "We are headed back to the dormitory at the nursing school."

I asked, "Can we walk you-all back to school? Just to make sure you get there safely." We all laughed. I was standing next to Mary, and Stan was closest to Grace.

Connie, Grace, and Mary looked at one another and said, "Sure, you can walk us back to the dorm."

I said that Stan and I were on our way to the Tandy Center. Connie said to Mary and Grace, "Let's walk by Tandy Center on the way back to the dorm. Since the two of you are not from around the Ville area, I can give you a mini cultural tour of this area."

We were having a lighthearted conversation; the chemistry was on point. Everybody was laughing and comfortable with the conversation.

Connie was hamming it up now. Laughing, she said, "Our Homer G. Philips's Nursing School basketball team will play our home games at Tandy Gym. I can see it now; the gymnasium will be packed when our basketball team plays our games there."

Mary said in a quiet voice as she was laughing, "I can't play a lick of basketball, but I am a cheerleader for the basketball team." Everyone got a big laugh out of that comment from Mary. Then I said, "I know I won't be watching the game as much as I will be watching the cheerleaders."

Connie said, "Willis, that sounds like you are sending a message Mary's way." We all laughed, and I said, "That's perfectly okay with me."

I think about the stroke of fate of Connie being one of the three young ladies that evening. As I put the four situations together that led to me meeting Mary Ann Byas, it reinforces my belief that there was a spiritual force at work for Mary and me to meet that day.

I have often replayed in my mind what happened that day: (1) I decided to go to Tandy Gym in September instead of October, as I normally would. (2) Stan and I decided to walk a different route, across Pendleton Avenue, to get to Tandy Gym. (3) Three fine student nurses from Homer G. Phillips Nursing School walked out of Billy Burkes' precisely at the same time that Stan and I were walking by Billy Burkes'. (4) I knew Connie, so I could be introduced to Mary.

It's highly probable that if I did not know Connie, the three student nurses would not have allowed Stan and me to walk them back to the nurses' dormitory.

Stan was walking and talking to Grace. She was very attractive, well-built and had attractive facial features. She was several inches taller than Mary. Connie was walking on the left side of Mary and I was walking on the right side of Mary. Stan and Grace were walking to the left of Connie.

Walking next to Mary created a situation where I could talk to her exclusively. Connie was positioned between Mary and Grace, and her conversation was uniquely between the two of them. The five of us took up the entire sidewalk space. The sidewalk was not wide enough for all of us to walk side by side, so Mary and I dropped back behind Connie, Grace, and Stan. We were now walking together by ourselves. When Connie introduced us and Mary and I looked at each other, I interpreted a special look and smile from Mary. I don't think I am stretching my interpretation of the look and smile I got from Mary. Her smile and hello were real and sincere; it was not imaginary on my part. I returned Mary's smile in kind, and she received my smile welcomingly.

As Mary and I were walking and talking, we got further behind Connie, Grace, and Stan. I am not sure if we were involved so deeply in our conversation that we were walking slower, or if they were walking at a faster pace than we were.

Ultimately, Mary and I were in our own private world; mentally isolated and oblivious to our surroundings. We were not seeing or paying attention to anything. We were not even conscious of Grace, Stan, and

Connie, who were walking in front of us. As we talked, we seemed to be compatible, without really knowing each other. We were comfortable talking to each other at this point; no gamesmanship being displayed.

Mary was an attractive young lady too. She was about five feet two or three inches tall and weighed about 115 pounds. As the expression goes, she was thick and stacked. I think what caught my eye most was that she had big, pretty legs. I thought she was very pretty. She wore her hair cut medium short, and she had a beautiful, beautiful smile.

We interacted as if we had known each another for a long time. Our conversation was flowing so spontaneously, it was as if someone was orchestrating the words between us. There was no male or female gamesmanship involved like there can often be when a couple first meet and are trying to size up each other. As we were talking, Mary told me that she was from East St. Louis, IL.

I was trying to make interesting conversation when I asked Mary in a rhetorical sense, "You want to be a nurse?"

As soon as I said it, I thought, *Of course she wants to be a nurse, dummy. Otherwise why would she be going to nursing school? Willis, that was the dumbest question. If you cannot think of anything intelligent to say, just keep your mouth shut.* Intentionally or unintentionally, Mary took me off the stupid block. Shaking her head up and down in the affirmative and with a determination in her voice, she said, "Yes, Willis, "I am going to be a nurse!"

Now I had my bearings again; so, figuratively speaking, I took the ball and started running with it. I told Mary, "I know you will make a wonderful nurse. If you had a sick patient, just looking at you would automatically make him feel better."

I heard Mary's muffled laugh, like she did not want me to know that she was amused by my comment. Now I was back in stride. I forgot about the dumb question I had asked her earlier. I was feeling the connection between us. We hit it off very well as we were walking and talking.

Weather-wise, it was a very nice evening to walk back to the nurses' dorm. We walked past Sumner High School, and I told Mary that I graduated from that high school last year. Mary said, "That is a big school."

As we turned the corner at Pendleton and Kennerly Avenues, we were one block from the Tandy Gym. The Sumner High School football practice field covered three-fourths of the block. Next to the football field was Tandy Center and it was the only building on the block.

It was now just before dusk. With the city street lights shining on her, I could see Mary's face and that pretty smile more clearly. We were approaching the retaining wall that kept the dirt from washing off the Sumner High football practice field when it rained. The retaining wall was a stone and concrete structure about four inches high at the lowest point, one foot wide and three feet tall at the highest point.

Stan, Grace, and Connie were still walking in front of us. I remember that Mary and I were having fun just walking, talking and laughing together. It was amazing because we had met just 15 minutes ago. Apparently Mary was feeling playful, and obviously she was acting a little silly too. She started to walk on the small retaining wall. To this day it just blows my mind how naturally comfortable she was with me from the first time we met.

Teenagers often try to act sophisticated; they usually cannot just be themselves. That is what struck me as so amazing about Mary. She was a down-to-earth, confident young woman who did not seem to have any inhibitions. As we walked and talked, I wondered if I was the reason she felt comfortable being herself. I was who I was all the time; an uninhibited and unassuming person; just a regular guy.

The retaining wall did not present any danger to her as it gradually inclined to about three feet high. She was walking with her hands extended out from each side of her body, like she was balancing herself on a high wire or tightrope in a carnival act. She was most certainly safe there on that little retaining wall. She was being very dramatic, laughing, and obviously enjoying herself.

Here was Mary and I, two mature young adults (I also considered myself sophisticated or hip), acting like young, delightful kids. It was amazing to me, and I got the vibes that it was the same feeling that Mary had.

Stan, Grace, and Connie all turned around to see what was going on. Apparently, they thought we were having too much fun by ourselves. When they saw Mary walking on the retaining wall they started laughing. With astonishment in her voice, Connie said, "Mary, come on now, girl. You are acting like a little kid. Don't embarrass me like that in front of Willis and Stanley."

We all laughed. Then, with a little attitude in her voice, Mary said "Connie, girl, I am not acting like a little kid! I am sorry if it embarrasses you that I am just enjoying myself walking and talking to Willis." I was smiling as I chimed in and said, "Connie, don't worry. Mary and I are doing just fine. You all just keep walking."

Laughing, Connie said, "Okay, I guess you told me." The laugher got louder as we continued walking toward the dorm at Homer G. Phillips.

However, as Mary was walking on that retaining wall, she was two feet higher than I was. In view of the illuminated streetlights, I was able to capture a full view of Mary's statuesque figure. I could see that, yes, she was fine! I was observing her physical attributes, her build, and her big, pretty legs most of all. I was taking in just how attractive she really was. I was getting a full view of this fine, healthy young sister. I was becoming impressed by her appearance, personality, and engaging conversation. Smiling to myself I was thinking, *Girl, you bad with your fine self.*

As I looked up at Mary on the retaining wall, my male player's instincts kicked in automatically. I was ready to put my move on her as I asked, "Mary, let me hold your hand so you won't fall from that retaining wall."

Without hesitation, Mary reached out and gave me her left hand to hold. As we walked toward the Tandy Gym, Mary was still walking on the retaining wall.

I had been holding her hand for about two or three minutes when we got to the end of the retaining wall. I asked Mary to give me her right hand so I could help her down from the retaining wall. She was laughing now. I don't know if she was nervous because the wall was higher at this point; however, she gave me her right hand. I took both of her hands, and she jumped from the retaining wall to the sidewalk. I helped to steady her so she would not fall. I have thought back on that precise moment many times. I honestly believe that was the exact moment when Mary and I spiritually and romantically clicked. The fact is, when I asked Mary, "Let me hold your hand," she held out her hand and I held her hand. I believe that connection instinctively cemented our future together.

I think symbolically and factually that was the fulfillment of my mother's vision that the Holy Spirit had shown her three times, three years earlier when I was 16 years old. It was confirmed several months later that Mary was that light brown-skinned, pretty girl that would be my wife in the future." At that time I didn't have a clue, and I was not thinking about marriage.

By the time we had walked the ladies back to their dormitory, I was feeling very confident. I thought I had made a fairly good impression on Mary, and the vibes that occurred between us were real. Therefore, I was sure that I would get her phone number so I could call her. I believe it took about 20 minutes to walk from Billy Burkes' to the dormitory. As I reflect on that evening, I certainly had confidence in myself walking and talking with Mary.

When we got to the dormitory, Connie and Grace said goodbye and went inside the building. Stan was standing on the sidewalk in front of the dormitory waiting for me. Mary and I lingered a little longer before she went inside the dorm. I asked her if I could call or come to see her.

Looking over her shoulder as she was going into the dorm, she said, "Yes, you can call me. My number is 456-7890." Then she stopped and turned around and with that beautiful smile on her face, said, "I will see how good your memory is and if you really want to call me." I saw Mary disappear into the elevator.

I rushed down the steps and asked Stan if he had a pen so I could write down Mary's phone number. Stan always kept a pen or pencil handy and sometimes paper. I found a piece of paper in my wallet and wrote down Mary's number. I put the paper in my wallet for safekeeping; I did not want to lose her phone number. When we left the nurses' dormitory, Stan and I headed home. I don't remember any personal information about Grace, not even her last name. Stan didn't see or talk with Grace after that evening. Apparently the purpose of the trip to Tandy Gym was for me to meet Mary!

Leaving the nurses' dormitory, I was hyped. As Stan and I walked home, I was jubilant, practicably euphoric after meeting and talking with Mary. Naturally I wanted to talk about her, but I asked Stan how it went with him and Grace. He said, "Lumps." I knew when Stan called me Lumps there was a philosophical discussion to follow. He said, "Grace was truly fine, but I just didn't get any really good vibes from talking to her. In fact, we really didn't have much of a conversation. For some reason we just did not click." He switched the subject quickly and using his hands to emphasize his point, Stan said, "Brother man," laughing louder and acting crazy. He was cracking up.

Still laughing, Stan said, "Lumps, I guess you were paying more attention when you saw me laying my game down than I thought." Laughing, I said, "Stan, you are a joke if you think I had to copy your game. I am the master." Stan was now cracking up, teasing me as best friends do.

He just fell out laughing, zigzagging back and forth across the sidewalk. I was walking with my best friend, and I could not wait to tell him about this girl Mary. After talking with her for 20 minutes, I had a feeling of excitement about her. My reaction of meeting Mary was the total opposite from Stan's impression of meeting Grace.

Stan and I were sort of comparing mental notes on what we thought about Grace and Mary. He said, "Lumps, apparently you and Mary hit it off big time. Connie, Grace and I didn't know what was going on with you two, but we thought that you and Mary must be having fun by the way you sounded. Lumps, were you laying some heavy rap on Mary?" Stan just laughed. He said, "It sounded like high-octane cooking behind us the way you and Mary were laughing. Grace and Connie said they had not seen Mary laugh that much since they have known her in nursing school."

Stan just continued talking as he usually did. He said, "Lumps, I can see you now tripping over to Homer G. Phillips as you leave the gym every night wanting to stop and see Mary. I understand you being excited, because Mary is fine too, Lumps."

Agreeing with Stan, I said, "You are right, brother. Mary is fine, and she has big, pretty legs. When she was walking on that retaining wall, I was checking her out one hundred percent. Stan, you know what was so interesting? We had a down-to-earth, genuine conversation. We were laughing and talking, and she is a cool, fine young sister. She is just a nice girl. Oh, excuse me, we are out of high school. So, I should say she is a fine young lady. We are young adults now, right?" That had a nice ring to it—saying young adults. Stan and I both laughed.

I told Stan, "When Mary gave me her telephone number, she said for me to call her."

Now it was my time to dominate the conversation, giving Stan the rundown on Mary and that she lived in East St. Louis. I said, "Stan I don't know how this is going to work out. I do not see myself catching the St. Louis Public Service bus riding across the Mississippi River just to check out a young lady, regardless of how fine she might be." Stan and I laughed as we were getting closer to home, still just shooting the breeze and talking about Mary.

As we were walking, I repeatedly told Stan, "I really enjoyed talking with Mary. In 20 or so minutes we connected like I can't recall happening with any other girl. I am going to call her soon."

Interrupting me, Stan said, "Lumps, be careful now. If you are too anxious wanting to call Mary, she might think you are a chump, brother man." He laughed, and I had to think a minute before I could respond. I just let it drop, because I knew I was going to call Mary sooner than later.

I was still excited and feeling good when we reached Taylor Avenue, we saw Cleart Jones, one of our running buddies. As soon as Stan saw Cleart, he started to finesse Cleart into giving him a ride home. It did not take much effort as Cleart said, "Come on, Stan save your breath. Don't tell me the long story. Just get in the car, man. I will give you a ride home." The three of us were laughing as Stan said, "Cleart, you are not going to let me give you my pity rap?"

Laughing, Cleart said, "Stan, I don't need to hear it tonight, man. Just get in the car. Come on, let's go so I can get back home. I have to go to work in the morning." Stan had a habit of detaining you when you were trying to end a conversation. Cleart started the car, and Stan quickly got in. Cleart drove off as he gave Stan a ride home.

I had to walk four blocks to get to my house. It would normally only take me about five minutes to walk home, but as I walked I was replaying in my mind the time I had that evening meeting, talking and walking with Mary Ann Byas.

I was in a relaxed mood and thinking about Mary as I casually walked home. I probably looked ridiculous to anyone who passed me that night. I was strolling down the street, and I had a smile on my face as I was thinking about this fine young sister, Mary Byas, who I had just met. I must admit that meeting Mary had a sudden impact on me.

The impression she made was one that I had not experienced before! Obviously, I was in a state of euphoria thinking about Mary. All of a sudden, I was home. I opened the front door and walked into the house. It seemed like I had literally floated in air, instead of walking those four blocks to get home.

As it turned out, Stan and I never did stop by Tandy Gym that evening. When we left the Homer G. Phillips's nurses' dormitory, we headed back home. Possibly, the purpose of me going to the Tandy Gym that evening was completed the way it was intended—not go to Tandy Gym, but to meet Mary Ann Byas, which I did in a most improbable way. I wondered about that reality many times over the years.

I slept well that night. At work the next day Cleart said, "Willis, Stan told me about the young ladies you both met last night."

Cleart had a naturally reserved type humor, in that he would start smiling before he delivered the punch-line or the major point he wanted to make. Cleart was now smiling, showing all his teeth. This was before he finished telling me what Stan had told him last night when he gave Stan a ride home. I was sitting at my desk just waiting for Cleart to finish the tall tale Stan told him last night, because I knew Stan had embellished it tremendously.

Cleart now had a sheepish grin on his face that quickly turned into a full-throttled laugh. Finally, he said, "Willis, excuse me for laughing, man. Stan told me that you walked this girl, I think he said her name was Mary, back to the Homer G. Phillips' nurses' dormitory. Stan said it took you-all about 25 minutes to walk them to the dorm from Billy Burkes'."

Cleart was now in a full-out laughing fit. He was shoulder-shaking laughing, hard laughter. Then he said, "Willis, you know I don't believe much of what Stan says. I know how he can exaggerate things. Anyhow, he told me that by the time you all got to the dormitory, Mary had your nose wide open."

Now Cleart was rolling as he could not stand up straight. I also had to laugh because I could picture Stan spinning that tale. I must admit that the way Cleart was telling the story was very funny. I got a kick out of hearing how my best friend Stan had portrayed the events from last night of me meeting Mary.

Cleart said Stan told him that when the two of you were walking home last night, he could not get a word in about anything because all I did was talk about Mary. Cleart was just rolling with gut-busting laughter. Then he said, "Willis, of course you know I did not believe Stan. He probably was exaggerating as usual, I'm sure, right?"

I was smiling, and I did not try to refute what Cleart was saying. I tried to make light of the conversation. I said, "Hey man, Cleart, you know Stan and his account of things are always exaggerated. I won't say he was lying, but it is close to really stretching the truth, very close to lying."

Now Cleart and I both were laughing, and I was laughing as hard as he was. I said, "Cleart, because I was not there with you and Stan to defend myself, you know Stan was going to blow everything way out of proportion like he always does. I did enjoy meeting and talking with the young lady, and her name is Mary Ann Byas. Man, she is fine. Did Stan tell you that?" We laughed more, and Cleart said, "Yes, Willis, Stan did say that Mary was fine."

Getting to Know Mary

My contemplating when to telephone Mary after we first met required balance. However, I was not going to be influenced on this point as to when I should call Mary, not even by my best friend who I would trust with my life. Within the 20 or so minutes after I had met her, I felt special vibes between us. Therefore, I was foregoing Stan's ribbing me about being a "chump" by calling Mary too soon. I was not going to let a stereotypical ego mind-set jeopardize my opportunity to get to know Mary Ann Byas better.

I don't recall if I called Mary the next day. I am sure it was only a few days after we had met that I called her. The old player's strategy of waiting a week before you call a girl you just met would give you an advantage to start the relationship didn't apply. Maybe if you were not interested in furthering a meaningful friendship with a young lady, that nonsensical immature approach might seem to be okay. However, I was not going to participate in any of that irrational stupidity.

For me that nonsense did not apply in this case. Mary had told me that she went home on Fridays for the weekends, so I called her before that Friday. I generally remember our first telephone conversation. It was a short conversation, and we basically chit-chatted about nothing particular as this was the follow-up to our first meeting. I remember telling Mary it was good to hear her voice, and I asked if she was surprised that I remembered her phone number.

She laughed and said, "Willis, it is good to hear your voice too. However, you know you wrote my phone number down as soon as I got inside the dorm."

I had to laugh myself. She did not go for the spill I just gave her. Still laughing, I said, "Mary, I do not keep a pen and paper with me. No, I committed your phone number to memory as soon as you gave it to me. Your phone number is very important to me. When you said your phone number, it was like an indelible image recorded in my brain."

I thought that comment would be impressive, telling Mary how I had remembered her phone number without writing it down.

However, this first phone conversation with Mary was much anticipated by me, and I think it was for Mary as well. Although Mary and I only talked for a short time, it appeared that our chemistry from our first meeting a few days ago continued with that first telephone conversation we had.

While searching for something to talk about, we chitchatted about how Mary's day went and how my day went also. I could not see her face, but

I could visualize that beautiful smile as she talked with the light laughter intermittently surfacing during the conversation. When we were getting ready to say goodbye, I asked Mary if she wanted me to call her again. Without hesitation she said, "Yes, call me around this time when I have finished eating dinner."

Then Mary said, "But it will not be easy to see me during the week because I have to study really hard to stay up with my class assignments. The best time to call me when I can talk longer would be on the weekend when I go home. If you want to see me, the weekends would also be better for me."

It did not escape my keen focus of hearing every word Mary said. She had said, "If you want to see me, it would be better to visit me on the weekend at my home." I was bubbling inside now. Twice Mary had given me the not-so-subtle hint or suggestion that I could come see her at her home. When Mary gave me her home phone number, I wrote it down. Then I told her that I was going to memorize her home phone number too.

Mary laughed and said, "Sure, Willis, you are so funny. I bet you have already written my number down." We both were laughing as we said goodnight.

From that point we had regular telephone conversations, probably every day or every other day, but they were always short phone conversations. That was pretty much our routine as far as me pursuing and dating Mary. Right after Thanksgiving, I told Mary that I wanted to invite her to meet my family, especially my mother.

As our dating intensified, our personal relationship grew stronger. I had never before had a serious relationship with a girl in the way that I felt about Mary. It was spontaneous the way our relationship was developing. Our feelings were flowing in both directions from me to her and back from her to me. It was like a cosmic connection. Something spiritual was traveling through the universe, connecting Mary and me as one. This was the first time I remember ever having such deep feelings for any girl, period; I never really got emotionally or romantically involved like I had connected with Mary.

It was Mary's Christmas break from school, and I had invited her to visit my home to meet my mother and family. When we arrived at the house, I opened the door and we went into the house. Mother was sitting at the telephone table in the family room. When mother heard us come in the house, she said, "Who is that?"

I answered, "Hi, Mom, it's me, Willis, and I have Mary with me." Mary and I were standing in the middle of the family room. As mother walked toward Mary and me, she was smiling. I asked Mother, "Where was everybody?" She said, "I am here by myself."

I said, "Mother, this is Mary Byas, and I am sure you have heard me mention her name a few times. Mary, this is my mother, Mrs. Drake."

They both said hello to each other. Mary's smile was as bright as Mother's as they acknowledged each other. Mother said in her normal friendly way, "It is so nice to meet you, Mary. Yes, Willis has mentioned you several times."

Mother asked Mary to have a seat on the couch and make herself comfortable. When I introduced Mary to Mother, I don't recall any unusual expression from Mother when she first saw Mary. It never crossed my mind about my mother's vision three years earlier when I was 16 years old.

I learned some time later that after I left to take Mary back to the nursing dormitory, my mother immediately called her sister, Ethel Mae Sanford (my Aunt Tee). Mother was excited to tell Tee that she had just met Mary and that she was the light brown-skinned, pretty girl that the Holy Spirit had shown her in a vision three times.

When I returned home after taking Mary back to Homer G. Phillips's dormitory, Mother was sitting on the couch with a look of happiness on her face. I sat next to her and asked her how she liked Mary.

Mother said, "Mary seems to be a really nice young lady. I had a good feeling about her as soon as I laid my eyes on her. I genuinely liked her right away. I think she is a pretty girl too." Mother did not tell me then that Mary was that "light brown-skinned pretty girl" that she had seen in her vision three times when I was 16 years old.

Mary and I dated for a short period of time. Her parents gave me their permission, and Mary and I got married on April 15, 1960. That was the most blessed day of my life.

CHAPTER 17

———— ◇ ————

Promoted to Technical Equipment Area

———— ◇ ————

ART McGUIRE PROMOTED ME TO a position in the Technical Data Branch working for Mr. Melvin White. That decision helped to shape the rest of my professional working career. The technical area was where the technicians made the highest salaries in the company outside of management. Melvin White was a branch chief and had two unit chiefs working under him.

Art McGuire personally introduced me to Melvin. I don't know what Art may have told him about me, but he was cordial when welcoming me to the branch. He discussed the work that was assigned to his branch and the work that I would be doing. He asked about my technical work knowledge and experience and also asked if I was familiar with the Federal Supply System. He said that Art McGuire told him I would catch on very quickly how to do the work.

I told Melvin that I had very little work experience with the detail aspects, but generally I was familiar with the Federal Supply System. I explained that I was proficient in reading and understanding blueprints and technical drawings. I assured him that I would be able to learn the job if I received sufficient training.

I had spoken casually with Melvin over the years when I had worked in my previous jobs. Melvin was a very likable guy in his late twenties. In general, he had a favorable reputation among all the workers. He had attended college for several years, but he hadn't earned a degree. From my initial observation, he treated his employees with respect and fairness. He was cool with most of the African-American workers.

When Melvin and I finished talking, he walked with me across the aisle and introduced me to Stanley Brown, the unit chief where I would be working. He was in his late fifties, medium height and somewhat overweight, with a rotund shape. When Melvin left, Stanley and I had a very short conversation. Then he introduced me to Charles (Charlie) Moore, who was the assistant unit chief.

Charlie was about 23, and he was an all right guy. I had seen him from time to time previously, and we would speak casually. We shook hands, and he welcomed me to the Technical Data Branch (and this unit). He said proudly, "This is the best performing branch (and unit) on the seventh floor."

I told Charlie, "I am glad to be part of this branch and unit."

There were 10 or 11 young men in this unit, ranging in age from 20 to 24 years old. I was the only African-American in the unit. Stanley Brown, my supervisor, was responsible for providing me with training for the job.

Personality-wise, Charlie was a friendly guy. He told me about my job and the work of the unit. He asked me about my experience in the technical area. I told him, that I was basically new in this specific technical-type work, but I knew how to read blueprints and drawings very well. I also explained that I would welcome all the training I could get to learn my job.

After we had discussed the job for about 15 minutes, he introduced me to the other members in the unit. I met Jim Heffington, Jim Pender,

Earl Lovelett, Jerry Rose, and a few more guys. I had seen most of them around before and had conversations with them.

After Charlie introduced me to both Jims, he explained that the three of them had attended high school together and were good friends.

Coming into the job without any prior experience, it was obvious that I was getting a break, just as many others had previously gotten. I didn't find the job to be that difficult. I thought the work would be routine for me had I received the proper training. Basically, my training was to read and learn the Technical Data Division's and unit's work procedures and documentation.

I had been working in the branch for three weeks when my supervisor, Stanley, came to my desk and unceremoniously gave me a pay raise slip. There were no comments from him about the raise. I know that the pay raise was directed by Mr. Hamilton and Art McGuire. I recall that shortly afterwards the situation occurred Stanley Brown left the company.

Shortly after I received that raise, the Daily Record Company lost their bid for the contract, and Mr. Hamilton was no longer going to be the project manager. Mr. Hamilton and Art McGuire had mentored me during the three years I had worked on the GSA contract. Now I would be without their support, and my work opportunities would likely decrease.

To this day, I still believe there was a spiritual intervention that guided Art McGuire's thoughts and actions in helping me to advance on the job.

I had been working in the Technical Data Branch five months when Melvin White was terminated for some unknown reason. A man name George Stephenson was hired to replace him. With the changeover to the new GSA contractor, I didn't have the same relationship with the personnel office. I don't recall that Art McGuire was the personnel administrator under the new company.

In the Technical Data Branch, I was able to fit in well with my coworkers. In general, they were cool young dudes. During the early months when I was struggling, they helped me. I was able to get up to speed and learn my job. I knew they had their own work to complete, which determined their job performance rating. We worked well together.

A Single Manager Concept for Department of Defense (DoD)

During the early 1960s, the DoD implemented a policy for the military service to create a single manager concept for the Federal cataloging system. This concept spurred the increase of processing Item Reduction Studies (IRS).

Under the GSA contract, the Daily Record Company and the Dale and Hammer Company expanded its scope to include working IRS for the Army Materiel Command. This IRS program was in addition to creating the technical manuals for the Army Materiel Command.

The Technical Data Branch was given responsibility for working the IRS. That was a large responsibility. The buzzword in the company was working AIRs (Army Item Reduction). The IRS were identified as AIRs. As a result, my branch chief, George Stephenson, assigned who he considered the most experienced technicians to work the AIRs. Once again, the assigned unit supervisor's idea of my training was to read the Standardization Policy Manual (DoD 4120.24-M) to learn about the Item Reduction Program.

With dedication, I immersed myself in reading the information on the Item Reduction Program.

Every day, as soon as I got to work, I would sit at my desk and continuously read the DoD 4120.24-M Manual. This went on for weeks. Reading the IRS program manual was like reading Greek. I didn't understand the information. It was foreign to me. The entire process of reading the manual became very frustrating. Any time I asked the branch supervisor a question, I didn't get a logical answer. There were several coworkers who would answer my questions and explain information to me.

I continued to read the IRS information in depth. There were many times when I would sit at my desk, and literally pray for help to understand what I was reading.

My Prayers Answered

I didn't have my mentors anymore and I felt professionally vulnerable. Week by week, it appeared that I was being isolated. Without my old resources, Ruth, Art, and Mr. Hamilton, what should I do? Then I realized that I would continue to silently pray.

I prayed for weeks. One day when I was totally frustrated and close to tears, all of a sudden, a light bulb turned on in my mind. I now clearly understood every word I had read about the IRS Program. Not only did I understand the information, but I could recite it verbatim, by page, section, and paragraph, from the Standardization Policy Manual (DoD 4120.24-M).

I don't know if it was the Holy Spirit or the fact that I had read the manual so much I was able to finally understand what I had been reading. It may have been that the Holy Spirit had opened up my understanding. Regardless, I know within me that my prayers had been answered. He always arrives on time.

I now understood the IRS information, policy, regulation, and procedures. I was confident about my understanding and knew that what I said was always correct. Without hesitation I was able to refute comments. When necessary, I could challenge supervision about the correct policy of the IRS.

As I started to work the AIRs, it became known within the company that if you wanted to know something about the AIRs, just ask Willis Drake. Dorothy Isom, the branch secretary, told me that on several occasions when George questioned the reason for some technical decisions, the technicians said, "Willis Drake said it." Dorothy was laughing as she told me that George was somewhat agitated.

Dorothy was a good friend of mine. She said that he was cussing up a storm under his breath and said, "All I hear is what that damn Willis Drake said. Who anointed him the authority on AIRs anyway?" Dorothy said that it was a humorous moment, even George had to laugh.

Dorothy told George that I had completed more AIRs than anyone in the branch. Dorothy also told him that Willis worked some AIRs that someone else had for over a year. Supposedly, they were so difficult to work, but Willis completed them in less than three weeks. She knew because she typed the transmittal letters that sent the AIRs back to the Army.

Not long afterward, George Stephenson got a job in Federal Civil Service as a GS-7. Many years later, a former coworker told me that George had retired from Federal Civil Service employment as a GS-11.

--- ◇ ---

CHAPTER 18

Teamsters Union Organizes Employees

--- ◇ ---

I THINK IT WAS 1962 when the Dale and Hammer (D&H) Company was awarded the GSA contract. I had been working for the Daily Record Company for three years, and had advanced to a meaningful technical position with the company.

Normally, employees hired for the technical job positions were required to have experience as a mechanic or equipment specialist in the military or have a technical background with years of work experience, or have earned a certification from a trade or technical school. My advancement at DRC, in the technical area, was unusual. When given the opportunity, I gained work experience on the job and became a knowledgeable, skilled journeyman technician, which allowed me to earn a reasonable salary.

My salary was commensurate with my coworkers. However, the overall salary for the classification of technical work performed on the GSA contract was below scale in comparison to the same work being performed at the McDonnell Douglas Aircraft Corporation in St. Louis.

Due to the civil rights movement in the early 1960s, opportunities for office jobs in the Federal Government sector and on government contracts were becoming more available to African-Americans. Overall,

Fairness and equal opportunity for jobs was being addressed with more consideration.

Calvin Parker, My Cousin

My mother's sister Josephine and her family lived in Memphis, TN. With Mother and our family living in St. Louis, MO, we didn't get to see each other when we were growing up. However, it's very interesting how strong our blood relationships were. When my cousins Calvin and Wardell Parker had graduated from high school and when Wardell had finished college with a degree in education, they each moved to St. Louis at different times to live with our family. My mother and father welcomed both of their nephews into our home until they could get employment to support themselves.

Ultimately, Calvin and Wardell were able to obtain well-paying jobs in a career associated with their education. My parents always supported family members who embarked on a journey to better their life's position. That is the type of relationship that existed within my mother's and father's bloodlines, their DNA.

Looking back, it amazes me how God makes a way for us and answer our prayers. During my parents' visit to Memphis in 1961, Mother's nephew, Wardell Parker, asked if he could ride back to St. Louis and live with them until he could get a job. My parents agreed and Wardell rode back with his aunt and uncle when they returned to St. Louis. Wardell had earned a college degree in education. He got a job in the St. Louis school system as a teacher. He lived with my parents for several years until he purchased his own home.

Two years later, in July 1963, my parents were visiting her family in Memphis. Mother's nephew, Calvin Parker, asked my parents if he could move to St. Louis and live with our family until he found a job. My parents agreed and effectively sponsored Calvin coming to St. Louis to live when he was 25 years old.

With the reputation and respect I had with the people in the personnel office, I was able to get Calvin a job at the Daily Record Company on the GSA government contract. Calvin gave me his written resume of his work experience in Memphis. He described his job in Memphis as a dead-end position. I took his resume and described the work he did in Memphis so that it would support the job position. I modified Calvin's application to reflect the correct "information" that the personnel manager would look for in Calvin's qualifications. I asked Arthur McGuire to hire Calvin for a job. Calvin started working for the GSA contractor during an interesting time.

From the GSA contractor's job, Calvin was able to have a successful and long Federal Civil Service career as a result of his own abilities, initiatives, and work ethic. During his Federal Civil Service work career, Calvin received numerous outstanding performance awards. After 27 years, working from 1966 through 1993, he finished his long, distinguished career as a Federal Civil Service GS-12 employee.

The Union:

Generally, friendships and alliances were being developed among the young white and African- American employees. This provided an opportunity to engage in a dialogue about the issues that existed on the job, especially issues that were unfair to the employees. Some of the young white guys in particular, understood what the rank-and-file workers had in common. The young workers also felt stagnated financially because the supervisors and managers were getting paid proportionately much more than the rank-and-file workers.

It appeared that the salaries of rank-and-file employees were not improving significantly on the GSA contract. Additionally, there were legitimate concerns and grievances of employees who were not getting a fair shake as they did previously.

Basically, the younger employees wanted to earn a higher salary to support their families. In addition, now it was difficult for the management to separate the goals of the young white and African-American employees with divisive tactics.

For approximately a year, there was a segment of the young white employees who raised considerable concerns about the salaries that were paid for the technical work being performed. Granted, these were valid concerns. However, from the African-American employees' viewpoint, there was a difference. First, the positions that were considered white-collar jobs were just becoming available to African-American workers. Among the African-American employees, there was a sense of having a fairly decent job, even though the salary was lower than the industry standard. Therefore, the African-American employees' viewpoint was slow to merge into the position of having a union represent the workers.

There were basically four divisions within the company under the GSA contract: the General Supply Division, the Aircraft Division, the Marine Division and the Technical Data Division. Overall it seemed that many of the young white employees working in the General Supply Division were cool. Their opinions indicated they were liberal thinking on most social issues.

The idea of joining a labor union started in the General Supply Division.

As the momentum increased for getting a labor union to represent the workers on the job, I couldn't help but to think back to 1959. There was an African-American lady named Ina Boon who worked in the typing pool. She had complained to management and the workers about how few African-Americans were being hired and that they weren't considered for management positions.

I am sure the same conditions existed then. Unfortunately, low salaries and some supervisors overstepping their authority and demeaning the workers could not galvanize the workers at that time.

Five years later, figuratively speaking, the water had finally begun to boil. Action was being taken to file for union representation on the GSA contractor jobs. It was now 1964. I am not 100 percent sure, but I think the main individual who got the workers to start agreeing to unionize the workforce was an employee named Larry Brumfield.

Larry was a few years older than me. He was about six feet, two or three inches tall, and he weighed about 260 pounds. I perceived him to be a louder-than-average person. In spite of his boisterous behavior, I think Larry was basically a fairly nice guy. He seemed to have established good working and personal relationships with many workers on the job.

Ironically, Larry Brumfield and I knew some of the same people because he had worked at an icehouse in St. Louis in the 4400 block of Finney Avenue in 1951. I was 11 years old then and lived at 4472 Finney Avenue. His uncle was in charge of the icehouse. The majority of the workers were African-Americans. Several of the men Larry named were the fathers of some of the kids in my neighborhood with whom I played. It truly is a small world.

Larry was also a good friend of a coworker of mine, Paul Bogosian, who, like me, was a former Golden Gloves boxer. Paul and I would talk and reminisce all the time. Gradually, Larry and I established a cordial relationship.

The overall social, cultural, and racial climate in the country was changing. As people began to communicate, friendships started to develop based on similar values and interests. I recall genuine male and female friendships forming on the job between whites and African-Americans. There were young people who socialized together, on and away from the job.

There was a group of young whites and African-Americans, male and female, who worked together, and they were really cool people: Kathryn Brizell, Jerri House-Schwarz, Herb Schwarz, Gordon Beswick, Paul Bogosian, Raymond Ax, Walter Hearns, Gaston Hearns, Joe McKinley, Elmo Johnson, Arthur Barham, Bill Barham, Caesar Herpers, Cecil Black, Earl Lovelett, James Mundy, Cora Henderson, Agnes Thomas, and Birdie Blackmon, just to name a few. They helped to create a cohesive atmosphere for everyone on the job.

The Vote to Join the Union

I started working on the GSA government contract in May 1959. There were approximately 400 employees who worked on the GSA government contract at that time. After four or five years on the job, I was one of the employees with longevity. Overall, I was perceived by the employees, particularly the African-Americans, as one of the most respected and knowledgeable employees at the company.

I don't know the terms of the D&H bid for the contract, but it seemed that low salaries and infrequent pay raises were conducive to having a labor union represent the D&H workers. The union meeting was carefully orchestrated. The sanctioned Department of Labor union meeting was held on a Sunday afternoon at the union office. At the meeting, a large majority of workers voted to have the Teamsters Union Local 688 represent the D&H workers on the GSA contract.

Also during the meeting, the employees voted to select a union representative for each of the four branches under the GSA government contract. My name was submitted as one of the representatives, even though I was not present at the meeting. The person who submitted my name was Ms. Jerri House-Schwarz, who said that she was sure I would accept the position. When the votes were counted, I had received more votes than any of the other three nominees who were present at the meeting.

I was one of four people selected to represent the employees and negotiate the details of a labor agreement with D&H Company management. I accepted the position as a union negotiator and a shop steward. My responsibilities were to meet with the company management and their attorneys to work out the appropriate job classifications, the pay scales for the various jobs, and other issues that were deemed necessary.

There was a learning curve in which supervisors and employees had to understand each other's responsibilities. Overall, I think the majority of the employees still performed their jobs as they did before the union representation.

However, there were one or two supervisors who, from past habits, wanted to perform technical research. Eventually that situation was resolved amicably. I had known and worked with the supervisors for several years, and they were okay guys.

Organizationally, the highest union official at Local 688 was the secretary-treasurer. His name was Harold Gibbons. He also was a member (I believe a vice president) of the executive committee that operated the International Teamster Union. After the union had been representing the employees for several months, there were social affairs, banquet dinners, and political activities that I was invited to attend. I attended the union social affairs with my wife, Mary. I could tell from various comments that I was being sized up by the Local 688 officials.

At union meetings, I was often approached by the older shop stewards, who had been union members for a long time. We would have short, polite, and friendly conversations. I felt that the union shop stewards were attempting to get to know me better. When I attended the monthly shop stewards union meetings, I got feedback from a few people, mostly African-Americans I had met at the union meetings. They told me that I was being viewed as a potential hire for the union staff. At that time, the union was looking to have a larger African-American presence among the union staff. On several occasions I was introduced to the Local 688 president, vice president, lead labor negotiator, and union organizers. However, I never had a desire to work for the union organization. When notable guest speakers attended the union affairs, I was introduced to them also. I remember having a short conversation with one guest, Bayard Rustin, who was introduced to me by the union president. The thing that I remember most that he said was "if you vote a person into office and he or she does no do what you expected them to do, then vote he or she out of office in the next election."

The Teamsters International Union Convention was held every five years. The union convention is where the international votes to elect, and install their president and other union officers for the new five-year term. Union members are elected as delegates to attend the convention. There was a union meeting held on the job to nominate two employees to be placed on the general Local 688 ballot, to be a delegate to the Teamsters Nineteenth International Brotherhood of Teamsters Convention in July 1966. It was held in Miami, FL.

The employees at the D&H Company nominated Richard (Dick) Stiger, the chief shop steward, and me to appear on the overall ballot. Dick Stiger was selected by the overall Local 688 membership to be a delegate, and I was selected as an alternate delegate.

There were three or four African-Americans at this event. There was another delegate from Local 688; his name was Tom Jordan, an African-American in his late fifties. I may have seen Tom once before at a Local 688 shop steward's union function. Tom and I hung out together the entire time we were at the convention. I saw Dick Stiger, the chief shop steward and my coworker, only briefly during the entire week of the convention.

There were many activities and events available to the delegates. I remember at one of the affairs I met an African-American newspaperman who lived in either Chicago or Detroit. It was apparent that the newspaperman knew most of the union people at the affair. Observing him, I had the opinion that he was trying to impress me by telling me that he knew Jimmy Hoffa very well. He asked me to come with him, practically running and zigzagging through the crowded room to where Jimmy Hoffa was standing.

When the newspaperman introduced the two of us, Jimmy Hoffa and I shook hands. He had a very strong handshake, and he gripped my right hand firmly. I told him I was a member of Local 688 in St. Louis. He said, "You are one of Harold's guys. Glad to meet you." We exchanged a few more words, and that was the only occasion I met Jimmy Hoffa.

◇

CHAPTER 19

GSA Contractors' Jobs Converted
to Federal Government Positions

◇

I DON'T RECALL EXACTLY WHEN the rumor started circulating regarding a major announcement pertaining to the GSA government contractor employees. The Teamsters' Union represented the GSA contractor employees for only three years. The biggest result of union representation was the conversion of GSA contractor employees to Federal Government Civil Service employees in 1967.

The job positions and classifications for the employees ranged from clerical to specialized technical jobs. The pay grades for the technical positions were classified as General Schedule (GS) pay scale. The grade levels were basically GS-5, GS-7, and GS-9 positions. Also, there were a few GS-11 positions for employees in management or administrative positions on the GSA government contract.

The job description for the job I performed was classified as a GS-5 position. Other employees who didn't have as much work experience or job knowledge that I had were given a GS-7 or GS-9 positions. The difference of two pay grade levels, GS-5 versus GS-7, was $1,250 in annual salary.

Initially, I was disappointed. When the shock had worn off, I was very upset that I wasn't treated fairly and given a higher GS grade, which I truly deserved. This situation wasn't unusual to me. In general, I was used to things being unfair, so I didn't let that issue linger with me for long.

When the jobs were converted to Federal Civil Service positions, I believe that my association with the Teamsters' Union may have influenced the decision of the GS-5 grade that I was given, instead of a GS-7 or GS-9 grade. I was a shop steward, an executive member, and worked on the employee's negotiation team that negotiated the specific terms of the union contract for the membership with the GSA Contractor. In my opinion, I was penalized for my association with the Teamsters' Union and representing the membership during the contract negotiations.

All of the GSA contractor employees were elated to now be working for the Federal Government. When I first started working for the Daily Record Company, the person I replaced, Michael, went into military service for the purpose of gaining an opportunity to get a Federal Civil Service job when he got out of the military.

Even though I was converted to only a GS-5 grade employee, there was an immediate sense of job security now that I was a Federal Government Civil Service employee. That same sense of security did not exist when I worked as a GSA contractor employee.

Over the seven years that I worked on the GSA government contract, I had built a reputation, based on my knowledge, integrity, fairness, and being honest and straightforward with people. I worked with people who would seek my opinion and expertise regarding technical issues concerning their job.

The standard process of getting hired for a Federal Government Civil Service job was to get certified on the civil service register. It was a national Federal register that evaluated your application (SF-171) based on your education, work experience, and technical or other background expertise. The Civil Service Commission Board would grade and assign a numerical ranking to your application.

With a ranking in the 70s, your chance of getting a civil service job was reasonably assured. My application had been qualified with a high ranking in the low 90s. My ranking on the federal register was graded up to a GS-11 position, under the classification of a Federal Supply Cataloger.

I still subscribe to the fact that when you are doing the right things, you will be blessed. I always tried to look at the positive results instead of a negative outcome. Regardless, some things are simply out of your control. Therefore, I always tried to be positive, and as my grandmother, Ma Dear, told me, just trust in the Lord God Almighty. That philosophy served me well throughout my lifetime.

I had done my part. I was certified on the civil service register as a GS-11. Now I just had to be patient. It was amazing to me to see the spiritual aspect at work. I only stayed at the GS-5 grade for one year! I was still working at the Mart Building. This is where the personnel officer, Art McGuire, told me that the day I walked into his office to apply for a job, he heard a voice say, *"Hire him."* Now I believe again that same source, the Holy Spirit, was interceding on my behalf.

The following year in 1968, I submitted an application to the Army Mobility Equipment Command (MECOM), located at 4300 Goodfellow Boulevard, St. Louis. The jobs at MECOM had been transferred from Columbus, OH. Some of the employees living in Columbus didn't transfer with their jobs so there were vacant positions available at MECOM in St. Louis. I was on the GS-9 and GS-11 supply cataloger register. My qualifications and also my reputation as a knowledgeable, experienced, and hard worker were well documented. These facts were known by the agency's management personnel, whom I had worked with during my career at the Mart Building.

When the GSA contractor jobs were converted to civil service positions, my supervisor at that time was Mr. Daniel (Danny) Morris, a longtime civil service employee. Danny was given a GS-9 position as branch chief. There was one GS-7 unit chief position that was held by Robert Vogel.

There were eight or ten GS-5 employees who worked in the branch. Neither Danny Morris nor Bob Vogel, the two people in supervisory positions, were sufficiently knowledgeable about the technical, policy, and procedural knowledge or the overall functioning of the branch's operations. As a result, Danny solicited my help in learning his job.

Throughout the agency it was well known that I was the most qualified individual for the branch chief position. Regardless of the fact that I was unfairly treated by the GS grade I was given, I didn't allow the decision that someone else made affect my relationship with Danny. I had an opinion as to why Danny, an African-American, was given the branch supervisor position, but I did not voice my opinion publicly.

All my life, I was fortunate to not have a resentful attitude toward someone when his or her actions caused a problem for me. I figuratively tried to turn the other cheek. That practice had served me well. As a result, I received more beneficial and positive outcomes than I did negative results.

I helped Danny as much as possible, to get him up to speed to effectively perform his job as branch chief. I think most of the people in our branch had a friendly relationship with Danny and Bob, but apparently, there was still bitterness, disappointment, and possibly even anger that lingered within them. They were not as generous with sharing their knowledge and information. Their feelings of being mistreated in the conversion process obviously affected their ability to assist Danny or Bob to learn their jobs.

I had known Danny since I started working at the Mart Building. Danny and I initially made a connection because of the St. Louis Golden Gloves boxing experiences we both had. During his teenage years, Danny was a boxer in the St. Louis Golden Gloves tournaments from 1938 to 1940. My favorite Golden Gloves boxing coach, Leon Hare, knew Danny; they were Golden Gloves boxers during that same period of time. Danny and I had many laughs about old boxing stories that he shared with me. After Danny finished high school, he went to the military service. I believe he was in the army.

Danny was approximately 25 years older than me and a great guy. Over the years, we had many enjoyable conversations as two African-American men. He would often offer me advice on how to conduct myself in the civil service arena and how to avoid some not-so-obvious pitfalls in the workplace.

He would say that, regardless of the times or the generation we are living in, there are certain situations that remained unchanged that I needed to be aware of, specifically regarding African- American men in the workplace. Danny told me that he realized that he had not advanced on the job as he should have because of the attitudes of his supervisors and their racial prejudices.

Danny was married, a devout Catholic and a very devoted family man. He used to talk to me about his faithfulness to his wife and the benefit of having a good marriage. He had a daughter and a son. His daughter was planning her wedding around the time that Danny became my supervisor.

Danny and I would talk often about many things, particularly about our common background as African-American kids growing up in St. Louis. We discussed situations we had encountered throughout our lives and within the government civil service culture. I know Danny thought highly of me as a young African-American family man. He would often tell me that basically all the African-Americans men and women working at the Mart Building always talked about what a fine young man I was. Danny was my mentor. He was mentoring a young African-American brother in how to navigate and survive the Federal Civil Service culture.

I remember vividly the day I went into Danny's office, and I asked him if he personally knew any of the supervisors at the Mobility Equipment Command (MECOM). I told him that I was on the GS-9 and the GS-11

Federal civil service register and that I had applied for a GS-9 position at MECOM. Danny said that he knew a former supervisor of his, Don Gaines, and he would let Don know I had applied for a GS-9 position at MECOM. Don Gaines was a GS-13, branch chief at MECOM. While I was in Danny's office, he called Don Gaines and told him that a person who worked in his unit, Willis Drake, had his SF-171 application on file at MECOM for a GS-9 supply cataloger position.

Fortunately, I also knew Don Gaines when he worked at the Mart building. Don and I had a cordial, friendly relationship, and we used to talk often. Don immediately remembered who I was. He told Danny that MECOM would be fortunate to have Willis come work for the agency and to expect a phone call shortly. At that point, it was just a matter of time before I received a telephone call from Don Gaines to interview me for the job. Needless to say, the telephone interview went well, and I got the job as a GS-9 supply cataloger.

Being hired as a GS-9, which was four pay grades above the grade that I currently held as a GS-5, was not normal. In fact, it was unusual. The normal progression was to move from a lower grade to the next higher grade, usually a maximum two grade increments. Getting the GS-9 position was a significant pay increase for me. My salary increased approximately $2,730 a year as a result of that four-grade promotion.

CHAPTER 20

◇

Hired at MECOM

◇

I HAD OFFICIALLY CHECKED OUT OF the Army Aviation Command on a Friday, and I was to report to my new job at Mobility Equipment Command (MECOM) on Monday morning. I was excited about reporting to work at MECOM. I had checked the Natural Bridge bus schedule, because I was now going to be riding the bus to work. Mary, my wife, was going to drive the kids, Willis Jr. and Monica, to Mother's house, and then she would drive herself to work. We only owned one automobile at the time.

Riding the bus to work was convenient for me. I lived near the corner of Natural Bridge and Fair Avenues. I could stand inside the entrance of my apartment building and see the westbound bus coming. I could walk out of the apartment building and be at the bus stop when it arrived.

The bus ride would take 25 minutes to get to Natural Bridge and Goodfellow Boulevard. I then had to transfer to the Goodfellow bus and ride about five minutes to get to the MECOM security gate entrance.

The MECOM was a totally different physical layout from the Mart Building. The Mart Building was a tall building, at least 12 floors, and MECOM was a collection of multiple warehouse buildings. There were at least ten buildings on the agency's grounds. The Supply Cataloging

Division where I worked was in building 103. Building 104 was where the requisitioning processing branch was located. I would have direct and continuous interaction with the requisitioning processing branch. In 1969 the Vietnam War was in high activity, if not in full force. Building 110 was the Maintenance Division, where the equipment specialists worked.

Building 103 was a one-floor warehouse that was the length and width of a football field. Upon entering the building, I had to walk almost the full length of the building to get to the Cataloging Division. As I was walking down the middle aisle, I noticed that there were two bays on the left side and one bay on the right side of the aisle. The desks were situated one behind the other. From the sides, the desks were very close together (basically no aisle space between the desks), but they didn't touch one another.

The branch chief's desk was located against the back wall. There were three GS-13 branch chiefs, Don Gaines(branch 3), Dale Borland (branch 2), and Mr. Denny (branch 1). I don't recall his first name. The cataloging chief was a GS-15 (named Jake), and the deputy cataloging chief was a GS-14 (named Bill).

I saw several familiar faces as I walked down the aisle to get to the cataloging chief's office. The secretary welcomed me to the cataloging division and introduced me to the deputy cataloging chief. We had a short conversation about my work background, and then we went into the cataloging chief's office. He introduced himself as Jake. Jake told me he had heard some very good things about me, and he was looking forward to me working in the cataloging division. Jake walked me out to the branch chief, Dale Borland, for whom I would be working.

When we got to Dale Borland's desk, Jake introduced me to him and then left. Dale Borland was a man in his mid to late fifties. He had a slender build, about five feet nine or ten inches tall, his hair was totally gray, and he wore a bowtie. At that point, Don Gaines saw me and came over to say hello and welcome me to the division. After Don Gaines and I had said our hellos to each other, Dale Borland called the section chief who would be my immediate supervisor and introduced us. His name was Bill Sorenson. He was a nice guy. He was in his early fifties, a heavyset man, and dressed casually, without a necktie most of the time.

Bill showed me my desk, and we talked for a short time as he went over the basic work guidelines and gave me some regulations to read. It wasn't long before old friends started to stop by my desk to say hello.

One person in particular who came by was Earl Lovelett, who I worked with and played softball with when we were both at the Mart Building. I believe Earl was a GS-11, and he was in with the management folks and those who had influence. Earl was a cool dude, and we had a good relationship. I considered him a friend from work.

I was just settling into the workplace and getting adjusted to working in the section of branch 2 where I was assigned. I had only been working at the agency for about three weeks when Bill, my section supervisor, came to my desk after lunch and said, "Willis, the Cataloging Division is in the process of creating a new special Requisitioning Processing Unit. I was told that you have been specifically requested to work in the unit. I hate to see you go and work in that unit, but I don't have a choice. You were requested."

I am sure Earl told George Spielman about my experience of working requisitions when I was at the Mart Building.

Bill said each branch chief had to provide several personnel to staff up this new unit. The Requisitioning Processing Unit (RPU) was headed up by George Spielman, a GS-11. George was a very intelligent and super nice guy. The RPU was also made up from some supposedly unproductive people who were hard-case employees that the branch chiefs wanted to eliminate. However, there were some knowledgeable and hardworking people in the group; in addition to George, there was Ardath O'Connell, a widowed lady in her late fifties who lived alone, and me. Her job was her primary interest. Ardath and I became very good friends, and she interacted with my family. She and Mary enjoyed each other's company and friendship. Ardath sort of adopted us as her family. She would attend Willis Jr. and Monica's extracurricular activities with school and sports.

The RPU was staffed with 11 employees. The operational organization was structured with one GS-11 supervisor, six GS-9 catalogers, two GS-7 catalogers, and two clerical and administrative support GS-5s. The GS-9 employees were Rick Poge, Annette Simpkins, Clarence Cox, Bill Houghton, Leonard Lenhard, and Ken Fox. Ardath and another lady named Jean were the two GS-7 catalogers. The clerical and administrative support employees were ladies named Virginia and Dolores McCadney.

The RPU was supported around the clock, 24 hours a day. Ken Fox worked the 4:00 p.m.–11:30 p.m. shift. Clarence Cox worked the 11:30 p.m.–8:00 a.m. shift.

Dolores McCadney and I were the only African-Americans in the RPU. I vaguely remember Dolores from our teenage days; her husband James and I graduated in the same Sumner High School class of 1958. Having Dolores to talk with helped me get through the tough times when I was supervisor of the RPU. On the job, Ardath was one of the employees on whom I could constantly rely.

This RPU was established and dedicated to working only requisitions in support of the Vietnam War. I don't know if it was George's idea to establish a unique working group to focus on processing requisitions that were coded high priority and that needed to be processed expeditiously in support for the troops in the field. George Spielman was seen as a rising star in the Cataloging Division; this opinion about George was generally shared by most people working in the cataloging division. He was extremely intelligent and fair minded. In general he was liked by the people who knew him. Those sentiments were shared specifically among the workers in the RPU.

After only three weeks as chief of the newly formed RPU, information circulated that George had gotten a promotion and was leaving the

RPU. George was promoted to a GS-12 section chief in branch 1. I had only been working at MECOM for about one and a half months; the other people in the RPU had more time in service and at MECOM than I did.

George told Jake, the cataloging chief, that I was the best person to take over the RPU. He said he couldn't recommend anyone else in the group who knew enough about the policy and regulations to function as the supervisor of the unit. In my presence Jake asked, "George, you know that group of people may not be the best collection of workers under any circumstances, and you think you want to shoulder Willis with that responsibility?"

George said, "I have worked with Willis for only three weeks and I am confident that he will do a great job. As difficult as it will be, he can handle the situation with the people working in the unit. Willis is a natural leader. He will be all right."

I expressed my reservations about taking over the supervisory responsibilities of the RPU, but I said I would give it a try if they thought I could do the job. I didn't have a problem with doing the work; it was if the people in the group would accept my authority. Jake said, "Willis, you let me know if you need any help with anything." Therefore, I was given the responsibility of the chief of the RPU, but I was not given a promotion or any additional pay for doing the job.

Initially I was opposed by some of the workers in subtle ways. I had to pray a lot and over time, I was able to get the workers in the unit to operate in a very productive fashion. Every morning, I had to report to the cataloging chief, Jake, regarding the number of high-priority requisitions that were open (not processed the same day of receipt) and when they would be completed. The cataloging chief then had to report the current status to the MECOM Commander (The General).

It was amazing how people's attitudes changed; with me just doing the right things, it brought out the best in them. I had some low moments in that job, to the point that I sometimes thought I wasn't going to be successful. At one point, the number of completed requisitions had dropped. During a meeting with Jake and the deputy, the deputy said that the branch chiefs couldn't get some workers to be productive, and it was unreasonable to expect me to get the best out of them.

I said, "I see a change occurring, so if the numbers don't improve to where you want them to be, you can send the function back to the branch chiefs. Give me two weeks." Jake said, "Okay, we will do that, because I know you have put in a lot of work in making this operation successful."

I had prayed about getting the people to be more responsible about their jobs. After meeting with Jake, and the deputy, I went back to the unit and had a meeting. I told the group about the pending decision—if we didn't improve our performance, the RPU was going to be disbanded, and they would return to their old work areas.

Surprisingly, Lenhard spoke up and said, "I have worked in civil service for going on 40 years. I never had a better supervisor than Willis. I know everybody hasn't done as much as we can do, including me. I don't want to go back to the branch that I worked in, where the section chief is on your back about everything." Lenhard looked at me and said, "Willis, I will bust my butt to make this unit a success." I didn't have to say another word. I had prayed that each employee would do their job the best they could, and that was all I asked of them.

After the meeting, there was a dramatic change in the attitude and behavior of everyone in the RPU. The number of completed requisitions increased significantly. Even more so, there seemed to be a stronger awareness in wanting to do the best job they could to support the military troops in the field.

I also had acquaintances and friends in the cataloging division who helped to make it fun to come to work. There was a collection of serious minded and playful individuals who balanced the work environment day in and day out. Some of the people had unique personalities that made talking with them enjoyable. I can recall a few people who were in the division during that time: Elmo Johnson, Earl Lovelett, Joe Hardy, Delores Owens, Harold Lee, Thesola (Jean) Starks, Shirley Cureau, Charlie Minges and others whose names I don't remember.

I worked in that job until I resigned from the Federal Government to work for McDonnell Douglas Aircraft Corporation in 1972.

CHAPTER 21

———— ◇ ————

Easton and Taylor Trust Company—Mr. Goodman

———— ◇ ————

I REMEMBER VIVIDLY ALL THE years that Mary and I were saving our money. We banked at the Easton and Taylor Trust Company Bank, located at 4915 Delmar Boulevard.

The bank was servicing a larger population of the African-American community during the 1950s. I initially opened a savings account with the Easton and Taylor Trust Company (Bank) in the mid-1960s. I didn't earn a large salary at that time, however, as a small kid I saved money in an empty glass mustard jar "piggy bank" that my mother gave me. I kept the bank in my top dresser drawer in my bedroom. After Mary and I got married, I would save the money first to purchase whatever we needed; we paid cash for what we bought. That was a habit I had practiced for a long time growing up.

When Mary was in nursing school, our living expenses were low and we were able to save our money. After Mary finished nursing school, we rented our first apartment. We furnished our four-room apartment with a complete living room set, two bedroom sets, and a kitchen set, including a stove and a refrigerator.

Mary and I had saved enough money to pay cash for the furniture. We bought our furniture at Lambert's Furniture Store in downtown St. Louis. At that time, it was an upscale furniture store, and we purchased quality furniture. In fact, Mary wanted this Italian-style couch, which was more expensive than what I wanted to pay. Mary insisted on having that couch. She said it was high-quality furniture and would last us a long time. We purchased the couch.

In reality, Mary was very prophetic; after 45 years, our daughter Monica wanted that couch. It was still in very good shape. Mary gave the couch to Monica to use in her house in Sagamore Hills, OH. Monica wanted to change the color of the fabric, so she had it upholstered.

After Mary finished nursing school, we opened our savings account at the bank. As our savings account continued to grow, I started learning how to utilize our personal savings account as collateral to secure loans from the bank.

In 1965, I went to the Easton and Taylor Bank to apply for my first bank loan. I was 25 years old. I wanted to buy a new Ford, a four-door custom sedan. It was not a luxury car. We just needed dependable transportation. The car was going to cost $2,200.

Mr. Goodman

Making a loan was an entirely new experience for me. There were several loan officers at the bank, and I was assigned to a man named Mr. Goodman. He introduced himself, and I told him that I wanted to make a loan for $2,200 to purchase a new automobile. Goodman asked if I had a loan history with the bank, if I had ever taken out a loan with the bank. I told him no; this would be my first loan.

Then he said, "The bank's policy is normally that the customer should have some loan history before the bank will approve a loan for that amount."

I asked Goodman what amount I would need to borrow to establish a loan history and the purpose of that bank policy. Goodman told me that having a previous loan in the amount of $500 would create a loan history record, and I then would have established a pattern to show how I had repaid the loan.

I told Goodman that I didn't think that a $2,200 loan was that large of a loan! I then asked him what the bank's policy and process was for me to secure the $2,200 loan with my personal savings account with the bank. He looked surprised and a little uncomfortable. I gave him my savings account number and asked him what my interest rate would be on a $2,200 loan for three years. That experience was my initial encounter with Goodman. I would have many more business transactions with him in the future. I obtained the loan using my savings account balance as collateral for the $2,200 loan, which I paid off well before the three-year loan period.

About four years later I secured a $20,000 personal loan from the bank. I used our bank savings account as collateral for the loan to purchase our first home. Goodman once made a statement that would have floored me had I not been sitting down. He said, "Mr. Drake, I don't know how you can do it. I certainly can't save money like you do. You own a nice automobile, you live in a nice area in the city, and things seems to be going well for you and your family."

Goodman repeated the question: "How do you save money like you do?" He continued talking, saying, with a puzzled look on his face and basically repeating himself, "I don't know how you can do it. I certainly can't save money like you do." I didn't think he was expecting a response, but he was looking at me as if he was waiting for me to divulge an unknown secret.

The way he was looking at me, I realized that he was expecting me to respond in some way. I thought to myself, *The audacity or impertinence of this man, Goodman, who has been privileged, compared to me, his entire life. He's asking me, "How can I still overcome (save money)?"* It felt like I could read his mind, thinking, *You earn a smaller salary, you don't get deserved promotions on your job, you can't get loans on your signature, you pay more for your food, and your cost of living is higher. So how do you get ahead and save money, living as well as you are?*

I paused a moment, and looking Goodman directly in his eyes, I said in a biting tone, "My wife and I both work extremely hard to earn the money we make. Therefore, we try to save as much of our hard-earned money as we can. We don't spend our money frivolously to make someone else wealthy. We try to save and use our income the best we can, so our family can live comfortably, and we have a plan for our children's education and their future too. However, my wife and I recognize that God has blessed us abundantly. Accordingly, we try to use what benefit we receive from our blessings, wisely and not foolishly."

Later that day, I stopped at my father's house, which was within ten minutes from the bank. I believe the conversation, or more importantly, Goodman's question was so mind-boggling that I had to talk with my dad about what he had said.

I pulled up in front of my parents' house, and Dad was sitting in his chair on the front porch. I walked up the steps and sat in the chair next to him. After speaking and exchanging a little small talk, I delved right into telling my dad about my conversations with Goodman. Dad just laughed. With a smile on his face, he said, "Willis, it's difficult for the white man to understand how the African-American man can do the things that we do when we are constantly confronted with a stacked deck against us. Son, just continue to be honest and trust in the Lord. He will continue to bless you and your family. That's how you can do the things you do, in spite of the hurdles and obstacles you have to overcome."

CHAPTER 22

$\diamond$

Working for McDonnell Douglas Aircraft Corporation

$\diamond$

I CAN RECALL SEVERAL CRISES that I experienced during my lifetime. However, it never seemed to fail that I was always spiritually guided through my perceived or real crisis. One being when I left my Federal Government job, and started working for McDonnell Douglas Aircraft Corporation.

In 1972, I was working at the Army Mobility Equipment Command, located in St. Louis. At this time, the Vietnam War was coming to an end. As a result, the Federal Government was downsizing the civil service workforce. The process to eliminate Federal Government jobs is the Reduction In Force or the RIF, action.

Military veterans, rightfully so, had preferential treatment for retention of their civil service jobs with the Federal Government. The pecking order for eliminating jobs included employees that were nonveterans; then length of service in Federal Government was the next determining factor in keeping your Federal Civil Service job. Therefore, the younger employees oftentimes were the first ones to lose their jobs.

In 1972, like many other employees, I received a notice that I was going to lose my job in accordance with the RIF process. I had no military service, and I only had five years of government service, which made me vulnerable to lose my job. The first initial RIF notification that I received notified me that I would be terminated in 90 days. Therefore, I immediately started to look for job opportunities in the St. Louis area.

The general comment that I heard was, "Don't be worried. This is just the first RIF action. There will be subsequent actions coming out that will rescind the first RIF letter."

I had worked all my life since I was a young boy. Regardless of what people on the job said, I had a reason to be concerned. I had a wife and three children and I needed to provide for their wellbeing.

The McDonnell Douglas Aircraft Corporation was one of the companies in the St. Louis area that utilized the same job skill-set, a supply cataloger, that I had working for the Federal Government. I also had some contacts at the McDonnell Douglas Aircraft Corporation, who were former coworkers at the Mart Building when we all worked on the GSA government contract.

During the RIF process, as individuals decided to retire, it made a position available for someone who had been designated to be terminated. Accordingly, the initial RIF notification often did change. In my case, my status went from scheduled to be terminated to having a firm job offer as a GS-3 supply clerk position.

Because of the uncertainty and the tenuous job position I had, even with a GS-3 firm job offer, I still felt very vulnerable. Shortly after I received my initial RIF notice, I had already started the wheels in motion; I submitted a job application to seek employment at the McDonnell Douglas Aircraft Corporation. I immediately received a response from the personnel manager, asking me to come in for a job interview.

At the same time, the potential of getting a better job offer from the Army Mobility Equipment Command was a high possibility. Accordingly,

I wanted to delay accepting any job opportunity from McDonnell Douglas Aircraft Corporation until I had evaluated all the government employment opportunities. I discussed the options with my wife, Mary. Leaving the FederalGovernment would possibly make me a little more vulnerable in the long-run, having less job security.

However, a job at the McDonnell Douglas Aircraft Corporation would pay me a higher salary than my current Federal Civil Service job. If I went to work for them, there was a possibility that I could return to Federal Government employment in the future, if I wanted to consider that as an option.

After Mary and I had seriously considered all the pros and cons of staying or leaving the Federal Government service, Mary deferred the decision totally to me. She said, "Willis, I will be satisfied with whatever decision you make. We have prayed about it, and I know you will make the right decision for us at this time. That's all we can ask for now."

I prayed about that decision long and hard; even then, it was not an easy decision to make. I had always basically listened to my inner spirit. Normally when I did that, I wasn't led wrong. I chose to leave the Federal Government in June or July 1972.

I accepted the job and started working for the McDonnell Douglas Aircraft Corporation. It was the first time that I actually negotiated the terms of my employment. I hadn't thought about negotiating for the job position before I went for the job interview. During the interview process, I realized that the personnel representative had a sense of urgency, and he seemed to desperately want to hire me.

Normally new employees in this branch were hired as hourly employees who were on a time clock. They were paid based on the number of hours they worked. Many of my former coworkers from the Mart Building, who now worked at McDonnell Douglas, were hourly employees. They had been employed at McDonnell Douglas for four or five years.

The salary employees were paid regardless of whether the office was closed for inclement weather or other reasons. I also had a savings plan or company stock share option that was different than the hourly employees. There were a few more advantages I was afforded as a salary employee that the hourly employees didn't have. The company also used a color-coded identification badge (ID) that distinguished the different organizational categories of the employees. As a salary employee, my ID badge was green color coded with my picture.

One coworker named Pendleton saw that I had a green badge and he asked how I was able to be hired as a salary employee. He said, "I have been working here going on four years, and I am still an hourly employee." I simply said, "I requested a salaried employee position when I interviewed for the job." The personnel representative agreed to my requests and hired me.

McDonnell Douglas had office space in the Northwest Plaza Shopping Mall located near Lindbergh Boulevard, St. Louis, MO. There must have been several hundred employees at that office location. The shopping mall was located about ten miles south of where I lived. It was very convenient for me to get to work.

Two weeks after I was hired at McDonnell Douglas, a friend of mine, Elmo Johnson, asked me about the job opportunities there. He went through the McDonnell Douglas job interview process, and he was hired as a salary employee also. He and I worked in the same department: our desks were located in the same general work area.

Elmo was three or four years older than me. We grew up in the same general neighborhood, graduated from Sumner High School, worked together on the GSA government contract at the Mart Building, and worked as Federal Civil Service employees for the Army Aviation Command and the Army Mobility Equipment Command. Now we were both working for the McDonnell Douglas Aircraft Corporation. We have had a long friendship over the years, and currently still do.

Elmo still lives in Missouri, and I live in Virginia. We talk on the telephone periodically.

At the McDonnell Douglas company, I worked as a supply cataloger. I was reunited with individuals who were former coworkers on the GSA government contract at the Mart Building in downtown St. Louis five or six years ago.

There were only a few African-Americans working in that office at that time. During this time, McDonnell Douglas was effectively improving their hiring policies regarding African-Americans in some of their offices and professional job classifications. The other thing that was unusual—I now lived in the same neighborhood as my coworkers at McDonnell Douglas. My children attended the same equivalent school district that their children attended, and my wife shopped at the same shopping mall or stores where their wives shopped.

Now I was part of the overall landscape of my coworkers, unlike eight or so years ago when we all worked in downtown St. Louis. At that time, I didn't actually know or realize that the cost of living for my coworkers' families was less than the cost of living for my family. They lived in the Florissant and Hazelwood communities or other similar neighborhoods, living in the county area as opposed to living in the city of St. Louis, particularly living in the St. Louis north side, the predominately African-American part of St. Louis. The cost of living in the area where we now lived was lower.

When I moved into the Florissant area, I found out that groceries were cheaper than when I lived in St. Louis. In effect, a fifteen dollar purchase at the grocery store a block away from my home on Mullanphy Lane in Florissant, would have cost me 25 or 30 dollars to purchase when I lived in St. Louis on Fair Avenue. Also, my automobile insurance was much less than when I lived in St. Louis.

I also was able to observe my neighbors and coworkers and recognize that their personal, family, and social problems were no different than the average African-American families. The difference was that the white community would conceal and prevent the publicizing of these types of problems, as if they didn't exist. On the other hand, certain personal and social problems in the African-American community would be highlighted and publicized in the news to indicate that these were problems unique to African-Americans. That was totally untrue.

I could observe problems with my white coworkers and their family lifestyles firsthand and up close compared to the reality that the white community falsely portrayed to the African-American community. It was a false image of them and their community. I could see for myself that the troubles and stresses of life on individuals and their families were equally distributed regardless of one's ethnic background or race. In other words, I saw families being dissolved because of alcoholism, illegal drug use, extramarital affairs; all of the problems that existed in everyone's community, regardless of ethnicity. The difference I noticed was that these problems were properly associated with the individuals who were involved with the issues and not made to be a broad brush including the entire group of all whites.

I don't want to portray myself as some holier-than-thou person, because I wasn't! I had the same human vulnerabilities and shortcomings as others. Time after time, I was strengthened spiritually during periods of vulnerability because of my faith. Basically, I believe that because of the type of person I am, I didn't stray far from my core character. I was able to be a decent husband and father. Additionally, because of the stereotypical beliefs of some individuals in the general white population, which included some of my neighbors and coworkers, I was committed to providing the image of who I was, not who the African-American race was. However, I understood that wouldn't be the case in the society and community where we lived. My neighbors would extrapolate any negative behavior or actions I did across the African-American perspective, instead of attributing my actions to me as an individual person who happened to be African-American.

I was a father who participated in his children's school, sports, and extracurricular activities. My son and daughter were engaged in the activities in their community, which happened to be the same community as my coworkers' children. There was more direct knowledge about the type of husband and father that I was. On the job, I always tried to conduct myself in a professional manner. I was very careful not to engage in off-color jokes of any kind. I didn't play at work when I should be working. I did my job, and I respected supervision and management; but I didn't grovel or act in a subordinate way.

As a man, I wouldn't tolerate or accept any disrespectful behavior from my coworkers or from individuals in management. If an inappropriate incident happened, I would address it immediately. I would confront whoever was involved, to make sure that what I considered inappropriate didn't happen again. I would nip it in the bud, as the expression goes.

From a qualification standpoint, I had extensive knowledge and experience as a Federal SupplyCataloger. In addition, I could read blueprints and drawings in a detailed fashion to extract the salient technical information needed to develop an accurate and correct description of items of supply to support the McDonnell Douglas F-15 fighter jet aircraft that was being provisioned and sold to the US Government, the Air Force.

I fully understood the beginning and end of the Federal Item Identification Description (FIID) process. I knew the rules, procedures, and policy for classifying an item in the correct Federal Supply Class (FSC) to prevent potential item duplication in a Federal supply catalog system. Therefore, at the McDonnell Douglas Aircraft Corporation, I was considered a valued employee.

My desk was located just outside of the department's personnel manager's officer. During the first year of my employment at McDonnell Douglas, I was assigned a few unique projects. I recall one project that required the owner of a company located in New York to fly down to McDonnell Douglas.

The company's owner didn't want to take a chance on his proprietary drawings being unintentionally compromised, so he hand-carried them.

His company policy didn't allow any company he was doing business with, including McDonnell Douglas, to have the drawings out of his or a company representative's eyesight. Those drawings were, in effect, the bloodline of his company.

Based on my ability to read and understand product and item drawings and blueprints, I was selected to work with the owner of the company in a secluded restricted area. My basic task was to meet with the company's owner, and in his presence, I had to review the company's drawings and provide an accurate description so the items could be properly identified as replacement or repair parts to be used on the McDonnell Douglas F-15 fighter jet. It took me approximately two and a half days to document the required item descriptions that McDonnell Douglas needed to establish a valid provisioning parts lists to be furnished to the Air Force as part of the provisioning contract package for the delivery of the F-15 fighter jet aircraft.

During my first year at McDonnell Douglas another situation occurred as a result of a government contract requirement that all the parts that were being provisioned for the F-15 jet fighter aircraft had to be prescreened at the Defense Logistic Services Center (DLSC) in Battle Creek, MI, to verify that the part numbers on the parts lists had Federal Stock Numbers currently assigned.

Ray Schnelting, the routine courier of the magnetic tapes that had to be hand-carried to DLSC, had such a frightening flight on his last trip from Battle Creek and informed his supervisor and the office personnel manager that he no longer wanted to take the magnetic tapes to DLSC. It was obvious that Ray was emotionally distraught from his experience and said he thought the airplane was going to crash.

I recall the personnel manager coming out of his office and saying aloud, in the form of a question, "Who can I get to take a magnetic tape up to DLSC in Battle Creek, MI?" Undoubtedly, Ray's experience on his return flight made the other workers skeptical of performing the courier's job. None of the longtime, older McDonnell Douglas employees volunteered, so I said I would take the magnetic tapes to Battle Creek.

I think my volunteering to courier the magnetic tapes surprised the personnel manager and my supervisor. The personnel manager's comment to me, in a questioning voice, was, "Willis, are you sure you want to do this?" I told him, "Yes, I will do the courier's job."

At that point, the personnel manager asked me to come into his office. He immediately told me, "You know that you will not only be representing yourself. You will be representing the McDonnell Douglas Aircraft Corporation. You will have to ensure that your actions are professional at all times."

Without a doubt, I felt certain that it was not standard protocol to make those comments; the primary reason he made those comments to me was because I am African-American. I told the personnel manager that his point was well taken, but it was not necessary. I informed him that I had traveled on prior occasions representing the Federal Government and knew how to conduct myself in a professional manner. I told him my personal character dictated my behavior. My conduct was controlled by my core character and by a much higher power.

Someone reading the account of my life experiences may get the opinion that as I encountered multiple situations throughout my life, I attached very strong spiritual feelings related to some spiritual intervention, guidance, or revelation.

After I had agreed to be the courier, the very next week I was asked to hand-carry a magnetic tape to DLSC in Battle Creek. I went home that evening and told Mary that I had to go to Battle Creek, MI, for at least two days. I had previously told Mary the story about Ray Schnelting not wanting to take the tapes to Battle Creek anymore.

Naturally, Mary told me to be careful and she hoped I didn't have the same experience that Ray did. That night I packed a small suitcase. I would get my airplane ticket when I picked up the magnetic tape at work. I flew out of St. Louis Metropolitan Lambert Airport on a large jet.

The air flight from Chicago to Battle Creek was a little over an hour long. The airplane had to fly over the lakes between Chicago and Battle Creek for a significant time during our flight. I believe the massive body of water we flew over was Lake Michigan.

It was early afternoon when I arrived in Battle Creek. I picked up my rental car went to the hotel where I would be staying in Battle Creek.

I called my point of contact, Kenneth (Ken) Longbottenham, at the Federal Center to let him know that I had arrived in Battle Creek. I told him that I would be coming to the Federal Center shortly, and that I had one pre-provisioning part number magnetic tape to give him from McDonnell Douglas. Ken gave me directions to the Federal Center. He told me to come to the Champion Street entrance, and he would meet me in the lobby.

Ken was familiar with processing the tapes. When he saw me, the first thing he asked me was, "Why didn't Ray Schnelting bring the tapes?" I told Ken that Ray's last return flight home from Battle Creek was very unpleasant and he didn't want to fly so soon after that flight. Ken asked me to tell Ray hello and that he hoped he would be able to get back to flying soon.

Ken and I talked for 20 minutes as we stood in the lobby of the Federal Center. He was a friendly person and I felt comfortable talking with him. He said, "Battle Creek isn't that large of a city, and it will be hard for you to get lost. You may want to take a drive and look at the city to consume some time, instead of just sitting in your hotel room."

Ken said it would take two or three days for the tape to be processed. He let me know there were a few nice restaurants in the surrounding Battle Creek area, and the hotel where I was staying could probably give me the names and directions if I was interested in going out to eat. Ken said he would call me when the tape was ready to be picked up. As it turned out, I only had to stay two nights in Battle Creek before the magnetic tape was ready.

The second day that I was in Battle Creek, not having anything particular to do except stay in my hotel room, I decided to take Ken's suggestion and take a drive through Battle Creek. I asked the hotel registration clerk for directions. She said she was more familiar with the area by the airport and she gave me directions on how to drive there. I left the hotel, still not absolutely sure which way I was going to drive. I started driving toward the Federal Center, possibly because that's the only place I knew in Battle Creek, besides the hotel where I was staying. Not knowing the city of Battle Creek, I didn't want to get lost.

Now for the phenomenal spiritual experience I had while I was in Battle Creek! As I was driving through Battle Creek, observing the neighborhoods, the houses, and anything unique in the communities, I suddenly heard a voice within my spirit. After discussing this situation with my pastor Rev. Dr. Marshal L. Ausberry, Sr. and obtaining additional information, I was able to discern that the Holy Spirit spoke to me, to my spirit. It was not an audible voice. The voice in my spirit communicated very clearly, *"You are going to live here soon."*

The experience of hearing a voice in my spirit when there was no one else in the car was puzzling to me. I wasn't afraid or startled, but I was surprised to hear that message from within my spirit. I looked in the rearview mirror to see if possibly someone was sitting in the back seat. There wasn't anyone there. I kept thinking, about what the voice told me, "You are going to live here soon."

Not being familiar with the city of Battle Creek, I drove carefully and stayed focused on the street names while I was driving. I wanted to be sure I could retrace the route; I didn't want to get lost. As much as I wanted to stay focused on the names of the streets as I drove, I suddenly lost focus. Immediately, I had a flashback to a conversation I had about ten years earlier with Art McGuire, which occurred about two and a half years after Art hired me.

Art shared the experience he had that caused him to hire me when I came to put in an application for a job at the Daily Record Company in April 1959. Art's words still resonated with me. Art told me that on that day, he heard a voice say two words very clearly, "Hire him."

When I think back on that revealing spiritual moment, I can only assume that the voice Art heard was within his spirit also. I know that the Holy Spirit completed the equation for why *I missed the bus, but I arrived on time*. Art McGuire was going to follow the instructions of the voice within his spirit and hire me for that job, at that time, at that hour, and on that day. He said, "Willis it didn't matter what you put on the application. I was going to hire you regardless!"

The situation that day provided several factors to be considered. First, it was obvious that since I had missed the bus, I wouldn't get to the Mart Building on time. Second, a means was provided for me to get a ride to the Mart Building at the right time. Third, that day it was necessary that Art McGuire be alone in his office. Last, two and a half years later, when Art McGuire revealed to me what he had experienced the day I submitted my application, I was convinced that the Holy Spirit was speaking to him on my behalf to get that job and to have a successful life.

When I drove my rental car through the city of Battle Creek, I heard the voice in my spirit telling me, "You are going to live here soon." I don't recall being startled like Art McGuire's reaction that day in April 1959, when he suddenly jerked his head straight up from reading his newspaper as I stood at the threshold of his office door.

However, driving through the city of Battle Creek 13 or 14 years later, I did have a very strange feeling. I was now wondering if I indeed had heard a voice saying, "You are going to live here soon." I basically just thought to myself, *That's strange. I really can't see our family living in this Battle Creek, MI, area.*

I also remembered a very close friend named Joe McKinley who often called me "little brother." In 1963 or 1964, Joe moved from St. Louis to

Battle Creek, MI, to work for the DLSC at the Federal Center. I recall that Joe literally hated living there for the two years he worked at the Federal Center. He eventually got a hardship situation declared on his behalf, and was able to transfer back to St. Louis.

Still driving through what I thought was the city of Battle Creek, I returned to reality and suddenly I realized that I had actually driven into, around, and back out of the city of Battle Creek. I had traveled through the city of Battle Creek, from one end to the other end, in less than 30 minutes.

There were adjacent townships connected to Battle Creek which enlarged the overall geographical area. I had driven through Springfield, Lakeview, and one or two more areas that encompassed Battle Creek.

Battle Creek was a very small city with limited social outlets, compared to St. Louis. There were very few grocery stores, clothing stores, or other shopping outlets available. There were no meaningful museums, places for entertainment, or other fun attractions for young preteens and teenagers. I don't recall there being any movie theaters in the city at that time. All in all, I didn't feel any apprehension or concern about my family and I living in Battle Creek. Maybe that was because I had heard spiritually, very clearly, "You are going to live here soon."

I drove back to the hotel. That night I recall still thinking about the voice I heard, and it wasn't worrisome. I didn't lose any sleep over what I had heard. I got up the next morning and had breakfast as I normally would. Later in the morning I received a phone call from Ken Longbottomham, at DLSC, informing me that the McDonnell Douglas pre-provisioning part number magnetic tape had been processed and was ready to be picked up.

I made a flight reservation at the airport in Battle Creek to fly to Chicago's Midway Airport with a connecting flight to St. Louis, at the Lambert Airport. I didn't have any uncomfortable or horrifying experiences on the return flight.

I delivered the DLSC processed pre-provisioning part number tape to the personnel manager; the job had been accomplished. There was no unprofessional behavior on my part that would tarnish or have a negative impact on the McDonnell Douglas Aircraft Corporation's image. It was pure foolishness, I thought.

When I returned from the Battle Creek trip, I had an important conversation with my wife, Mary. I told her of the revelation I had driving through the city of Battle Creek, when a voice spoke to me in my spirit, stating, "You are going to live here soon." I told Mary that I was still puzzled about the experience."

Mary's only response was, "Willis, that is something!" I asked Mary, "Do you think you would like to live in Battle Creek? I said I will just trust in the Lord God Almighty!" Mary said, "We will wait and see what happens next."

Mary and I both laughed as I told her of the limited access to shopping in Battle Creek. Still laughing, I said, "Battle Creek may be a good place for us. We may save money because you won't have any place to shop and spend money."

Mary stopped laughing, and with a sarcastic tone, she said, "Willis, do you want to bet?" With a little more serious look on her face, she said, "Now Willis, don't be silly. You know I will find someplace to shop wherever we live."

We both laughed as I took her in my arms and gave her a tight hug. I'm not sure that we had any further discussions about moving to Battle Creek in the following months.

At that time, I had been working at McDonnell Douglas for about a year. Organizationally, the company had multiple departments, and employed a large number of people in the St. Louis area. I came to work as usual one morning, and there was a new employee in the office. His name was Sam. He had 19 years of service with McDonnell Douglas.

He had worked in a department that was cutting back its staff and laying off workers. As a result, he was transferred to our office.

Sam didn't dress in the traditional attire of a shirt, tie, and suit or sport jacket. He wore a black leather jacket and jeans, and he rode a motorcycle to work. Sam's desk was next to mine, and it seemed that I was one of the few people in the office who talked to him. We were talking one day when he told me that because of the number of years he had with the company, management gave him a temporary job for 30 days in our department to see if they could find another permanent position for him instead of laying him off.

After talking with Sam, I can still remember the thoughts that circulated through my mind. Within that short timeframe of talking with Sam, the future of my family flashed boldly in front of me. A justifiable fear came over me regarding my long-term future job security.

When I got home, the concern I had was still pressing heavily on my consciousness. Trying to push the negative thoughts from my mind, I got dinner started. All the time I was thinking about what life would hold for our family 20 years down the road if I ended up in Sam's situation.

Mary walked into the house, giving her familiar greeting, "Hey, babe."

I called out and said, "Hi, Mary." I told Willis Jr. and Monica, "Your mother is home. Let's get ready for dinner."

Mary came into the kitchen and said, "That smells good. What did you fix?"

She gave me a kiss, and I said, "I cooked what you put out this morning for me to fix. Why don't you wash up? I'm hungry now, and I don't want the food to get cold."

After Mary and Monica had cleaned up the kitchen, Willis Jr. was practicing his trumpet lesson. Shortly afterward, Mary and I went into our bedroom, and I started talking to her about the insecurity I now felt working at McDonnell Douglas. I told her of the conversation I had that morning with Sam and how I had been thinking all day about the fact that I only had a little over one year of service with the company and about the job security I would have 20 years down the road. With 19 years of service with the company, Sam was most likely going to be without a job in 30 days.

I said, "Baby, I don't see a secure future for me at McDonnell Douglas if they would let a person go with 19 years of service and keep me, when I have less than two years of service with the company." I think that Sam's situation, more than anything, is what motivated me to seek getting back into the Federal Government.

There were government contracting officers or contractor administrators who had oversight of the McDonnell Douglas contract. There were government employees with the standard GS- series classifications, pay grades, and appropriate titles. There were three or four government civil service workers physically located at McDonnell Douglas where I was working. The head of the government contracting office was a GS-11 or GS-12 supply cataloger position. I had been working at McDonnell Douglas for almost a year when a GS-9 supply cataloger position came open in the government contracting office. Many of the employees within our office who previously had worked together at the Mart Building as supply catalogers were thinking about applying for that job opening.

Several McDonnell Douglas workers, including myself, applied for the position. Another employee named Jim Heffington, who had previously worked with me at the Mart Building for five or six years, also applied for the position.

Jim was a knowledgeable supply cataloger. As I recall, he was a conscientious, hardworking, and dedicated worker as well. Jim was about 36 years old, two or three years older than me. Over the years, when we were colleagues on the GSA government contract, we both periodically played pickup baseball games with a group of fellow workers.

I admitted to Mary that I had strongly hoped that I would get that government civil service GS-9 supply cataloger job at McDonnell Douglas. That seemed to be ideal for us.

Through the grapevine, I heard that Jim Heffington was selected for the position. I was officially informed that I wasn't selected for the job. For some reason, I wasn't disappointed; I was okay knowing that Jim was selected for the job.

The kitchen table is where we mostly talked about the concerns or issues of the day, as well as the things that happened with Willis Jr. and Monica at school. It was our routine to discuss everything that affected our family before we decided on any course of action.

That evening I let Mary know that Jim Heffington, who I believe she had met before, was selected for the GS-9 supply cataloger position. Mary asked me if I was terribly disappointed that I didn't get the job. I said, "Mary, baby, I hoped that I would get the job, but for some reason, I'm not upset that I didn't get the job."

I also told Mary that I was going to submit applications at several Federal agencies that had positions open for which I was qualified. I explained to her that I wanted to get back into the Federal Government, where I would have more job security.

That night, in our bedroom, with Mary sitting in a chair and me sitting on the side of the bed, we talked in detail about what would happen if I was hired for one of the positions and we would have to relocate to a new city and state outside the St. Louis area.

Mary, with her always-supportive attitude, got up from her chair, smiling, and leaned down to me, sitting on the side of the bed. She put her face close to mine. Her actions took me back to the very first time I had visited her at Homer G. Phillips' nurse's dormitory, when she did the same thing. She now put her arms around my neck and kissed me.

Then she said, with such confidence, "That will not be a problem, baby, if we have to relocate to a different city. If that's what it will take for us to obtain long-term security in providing for our family in the future, so be it!"

Mary said, "I will go wherever a new job opportunity takes you. I am sure, at their ages, moving wouldn't be a big problem for the children to make new friends and get adjusted to a new community either."

I told Mary that I had researched some job announcements with several Federal agencies, and I would have an opportunity to work for the Federal Government again, potentially in one of three cities: Des Moines, IA; Rock Island, IL; and Battle Creek, MI.

I asked if she preferred one of the cities over the other two. She said, "I really don't know much about any of those three cities, but I know Des Moines is a college town, and it may have some educational, social, cultural, shopping, and entertainment outlets that could enrich our lives."

I told Mary that I would submit my job application to the individual Federal agencies in all three of those locations, and we would just wait to see what job offers I got.

I had been working at McDonnell Douglas for about year and a half when I submitted my application to the three Federal agencies. I thought that my Federal job application and my resume overall was very impressive. I had roughly 12 years of experience in the Federal supply cataloging field. I had strong documented performance at every level of job that I had worked, both within the Federal Government as well as in the private sector.

Additionally, with my reinstatement rights to Federal Government Civil Service employment, along with my work experience, I was confident that I should rank high for the jobs for which I had applied. That combination most likely made me a prime candidate to be selected for one of the Federal jobs.

Ultimately, within the same timeframe, I got positive job offers from both Des Moines, IA, and Rock Island, IL. However, both job offers were for a GS-5 grade level position. About a week later, I got a response from the Defense Logistics Service Center (DLSC) in Battle Creek, MI. The response from their personnel office stated that my application qualified me for a GS-9 supply cataloger position and was being reviewed for consideration.

The Fourth Blessing

It was late March or early to mid-April 1974 when I started receiving responses from the Federal agencies where I had submitted my job applications. I want to reiterate what I associated with having a guardian angel. This time, there was no verbal, mental, or spiritual notification regarding the job selection that was awarded to another individual, Richard (Dick) Ferrari.

Jerry Rose was a former coworker from the Mart Building during the mid-1960s. Jerry started working for McDonnell Douglas approximately five or six years before I started working there. Therefore, it had been at least five years since I last saw Jerry. I had difficulty imagining that Jerry would appear at my desk after that length of time without a spiritual intervention. I had been working at McDonnell Douglas for a year and a half and he had not stopped by to see me as other former coworkers from the Mart Building had done.

The primary reason that Jerry Rose stopped by my desk was to tell me that Dick Ferrari had been picked up for a Federal Government Civil Service GS-9 supply cataloger job in Battle Creek, MI.

Jerry and Dick were two of the young guys I used to play softball and baseball with when we worked at the Mart Building. Jerry also said Dick had to leave immediately to start work at DLSC on Monday of the next week and there was no time to have a going-away party for Dick.

To me, that had to be more than just a happenstance that caused Jerry, whom I hadn't seen in five or six years, to stop by my desk and tell me that Dick had been selected for the job in Battle Creek, MI. Jerry did not know I had also applied for that job.

My thinking on this spiritual act was fortified by the following actions.

Battle Creek was the city I had traveled to twice when working for McDonnell Douglas. I had personally couriered a magnetic tape to be processed at DLSC.

The future was forecast when I traveled to Battle Creek the very first time. I had a spiritual revelation during my first visit. This spiritual revelation came to me in the form of a voice touching my spirt, informing me, "You are going to live here soon."

I had prayed for an opportunity to get back into Federal Government Civil Service employment.

Basically, I wouldn't have known that Dick Ferrari was selected for the same GS-9 supply cataloger position that I had applied for if Jerry Rose hadn't stopped by my desk and told me the news.

When you apply for a job with the Federal Government, the normal procedure is that agency will notify you that you are not qualified or that you are qualified, but you were not selected for the job. In my case, I would not have known who was selected for the job.

Dick and I had worked together at the US Army Aviation Command located in the Mart Building in downtown St. Louis. We also worked together at the Army Mobility Equipment Command in St. Louis. I knew Dick's work background reasonably well. He was a cool and very cordial guy. Periodically, we interacted sociably after softball games.

I also knew that Dick resigned from his civil service job before he had completed three years of service in the Federal Government. Therefore, he didn't have automatic reinstatement rights. More accurately, Dick most certainly didn't have reinstatement rights over someone with reinstatement rights, as I did.

So again, here's another example of why I stated that there had to be a spiritual factor involved for Jerry to stop by my desk. Basically, Jerry was the messenger to let me know that Dick had been selected for the job at DLSC in Battle Creek.

As soon as Jerry told me that Dick was hired for a job in Battle Creek, my mind was propelled into activity mode. When Jerry left my desk, I immediately went to the public telephone located in the hallway outside of my work area. I was wondering to myself just how it was that Jerry had stopped by my desk after five or six years to let me know Dick had been hired for a job in Battle Creek.

I was aware of the Federal regulation regarding reinstatement rights for former Federal Civil Service employees. With this knowledge, I called the DLSC personnel office in Battle Creek. I asked to speak with the personnel representative who was handling the application review process for the GS-9 supply cataloger position that was advertised.

I may have spoken to one or two individuals before I was transferred to Ms. Geraldine Smith, the personnel manager or supervisor in the office. I identified myself and explained that I was interested in the status of the GS-9 supply cataloger position for which I had applied. Ms. Smith told me that she had overseen the applicants' qualifications review process. She stated that the ranking for the applications had been scored in order to select the top three applicants to be considered for an interview.

Ms. Smith told me the top three applications had been forwarded to the selecting supervisor who made the hiring selection for the GS-9 supply cataloger position. I listened intently as Ms. Smith explained the job selection process to me.

After listening to everything Ms. Smith had said, I restated my name. I said that I was Willis Drake and I had submitted an application (SF-171) for the GS-9 supply cataloger position. I also stated that the job had been advertised as an open vacancy at DLSC. I informed her that I was just checking to see if I qualified for the job and the current status of the selection for the position. Ms. Smith replied that she remembered reviewing my application and how impressive it was. She shared that my application was one of the top three that was submitted to the supervisor for consideration for the GS-9 supply cataloger position.

I asked Ms. Smith if she knew who was or would be selected for the job. I could hear in her voice the congenial reply to my question. She told me, in sort of a congratulatory response, that I was one of the very highly qualified applicants for the position. However, there was someone else equally qualified for the position, and that's who the selecting supervisor had selected for that GS-9 supply cataloger job.

I paused for what felt like a minute. I then asked her if she knew the name of the person who was selected for the job. She told me without hesitation that Richard Ferrari was selected for the job.

Immediately, I responded that I knew Richard Ferrari and that we used to work together at the Mobility Equipment Command in Saint Louis, MO. Before Ms. Smith could respond, I then informed her that I knew Dick didn't have automatic Federal Government Civil Service reinstatement rights because he had left Federal Government service before completing the mandatory three years of consecutive government service. There was a silence on the other end of the telephone. I started to talk again to break the silence.

I told Ms. Smith that I did have automatic or preferential reinstatement rights over anyone without reinstatement rights, including preferential reinstatement rights to the job for which Richard Ferrari and I were both competing. There was silence again on the other end of the telephone, as if Ms. Smith had lost her concentration for a moment.

When she collected herself, and she said, "There is another job for a GS-9 supply cataloger position that I am certain, looking at your SF-171 application, you would be qualified for. In fact, I can't see any reason why you would not be selected for that position. The position is in the NATO (North Atlantic Treaty Organization) Cataloging Division. You should expect to receive a telephone call within the week for an interview with the selecting supervisor for that GS-9 supply cataloger position."

It was all I could do to contain myself. I had this joy bubbling up inside me from Ms. Smith acknowledging that she was certain I would be selected for the available GS-9 supply cataloger position in the NATO area. I went back to my work area and had extreme difficulty focusing on my job. I could only think about the fact that my prayers had been answered. I was going to get a job that would return me to Federal Government employment.

It was a standard practice for Mary and I not to call each other on the job unless it was an emergency situation. Therefore, I waited all day to tell Mary the good news that I had been selected for the job in Battle Creek.

I always got home before Mary and usually I would start preparation for our dinner. I don't recall what we had for dinner that day. However, Monica did her usual chores of helping to set the dinner table so we could eat dinner when Mary got home.

When Mary got home, I planned to gradually tell her the good news. I hadn't decided if I was going to tell Willis and Monica during dinner about us moving. We usually kept the kids updated on things that affected our family overall. The normal practice was to include them in family discussions during dinnertime as a method of ensuring we had a close-knit family unit. Because we were isolated in a predominately white community, we involved our kids in most of the information we talked about in our household.

When Mary got home, we had our normal pleasantries, greeting each other. Then after Mary mussed and fussed over Kermit Matthew, she washed her hands, and we sat down to have dinner. As usual, we had the kids tell us about their day, but they didn't have anything overwhelming to share. Mary, smiling, stated that she had a good day; nothing unusual happened; it was just a very good day. Willis Jr. and Monica were still at the kitchen table. I began to tell Mary directly about the telephone conversation I had earlier in the day, when I found out about the job I had applied for in Battle Creek. Mary was very excited to hear the news that I got the job. She was smiling from ear to ear as she told me that she knew all along that I was going to get one of the jobs to get back in the Federal Government. We both were extremely happy.

Willis Jr. asked, "What does that mean? Will we have to move?"

It's strange how things work out sometimes. The family across the street from us, whose kids (Mary and Ronnie Schumacher) played with Willis Jr. and Monica every day, had just told them that they were moving back to Nebraska. The fact that the Schumacher's were moving lessened the impact of our kids having to move out of state too.

However, I cautioned Mary that we should contain our excitement and joy until the actual telephone interview scheduled for the next week, and then Mary said, "Okay, but I am going to rejoice now, because I already know you have the job."

Willis Jr., and Monica weren't as excited as Mary and I. Of course, Kermit Matthew did not understand the impact of us having to move. I told the kids that we would talk more next week about what all this meant.

Received a Job Offer from the Defense Logistics Services Center in Battle Creek

I received a telephone call from the supervisor and branch chief of the NATO Cataloging General Supply Branch. Her name was Ms. Johno Gailey. She immediately let me know that she had reviewed my job application and was impressed with my background and work experience. She asked me a series of general questions regarding the Federal cataloging system. The length of the interview was approximately twenty minutes. At the end of the interview, Ms. Gailey asked me if I would accept the GS-9 supply catalog position she had available in the NATO General Supply Cataloging Branch.

She also asked, if I accepted the position, when could I report to work?

I told Ms. Gailey, "Yes, I will accept the job, and I can report to work in three weeks."

My prayers had been answered. Without a question. I am certain that each step of the process of being reinstated to the Federal Government workforce was the result of the Holy Spirit. It started with me hearing the voice in my spirit, "You are going to live here soon."

That day, as usual, I got home about an hour before Mary arrived home. When Mary walked in the house and saw me, she said, "You got the job, didn't you!" I was smiling, and I told her yes and that my job interview went very well. As Mary and I talked, the reality was setting in that we were leaving both of our parents and our families behind in the place we had called home all our lives.

Moving from St. Louis to Battle Creek

I told Mary that I had to move to Battle Creek in three weeks. Therefore, it would be seven weeks before I could relocate her and the kids to Battle Creek. It would be in June, when school would be out, before Mary and the family could move.

When I went to Battle Creek, Mary had to take care of every detail of managing the household without my help. In every case with Mary, she would martial up the resolve to make sure everything was well taken care of.

We had many preparations to make before we could move to Battle Creek. I contacted my friend Cecil Black; he had moved with his wife Jerri and their three-year-old son, Kenneth (Kenny), to Battle Creek a year earlier. They lived in Lakeview, MI, a community about three miles outside of Battle Creek.

After I moved to Battle Creek, Mary and I would talk every night. When we talked on the phone, she would always tell me about the positive things that she was able to accomplish that day. She did not complain if she had a bad day, unless it was totally overwhelming for her.

Finally, June had arrived and school was out. I now headed home to move Mary and the kids to Battle Creek. My plane was scheduled to depart the airport about five o'clock in the evening. I believe my plane was due to arrive in St. Louis about 7:30 p.m.. I remember arriving at the house. When I entered, it was a very emotional and happy time for Mary and the kids. They had unbelievable smiles on their faces, and I knew they had missed me the same as I had missed them. It was great to put my arms around Mary and hug the kids.

It was a very short evening because we were going to leave early the next morning to drive to Battle Creek. Mary's brother David was going to help us drive our car and the U-Haul truck to Battle Creek. He also was going to help us unload the truck and put the furniture in our apartment when we arrived in Battle Creek.

It was an eight-hour drive to Battle Creek. In spite of having to move from St. Louis, the kids enjoyed the trip to their new home. We had a safe journey there. I had told the kids that when we reached Kalamazoo, MI we would be only 20 minutes from Battle Creek.

When we passed Kalamazoo, we arrived at the apartment complex of Fort Custer. When we went into the apartment, as was our routine when we moved into a new house, we took our Bible and formed a circle, holding each other's hands. Then we prayed that our new home would be blessed. We thanked God for allowing us to arrive at our new home safely and that we would have a wonderful life in Battle Creek.

Cecil and Jerri Black met us at the apartment to help us unload the truck. We finished unloading the truck that evening. A successful move of our family from St. Louis to Battle Creek was complete! I know the Holy Spirit had guided our directions from the time that I was informed by the Holy Spirit, "You are going to live here soon."

Our family got settled in our new community, Springfield, MI, which was located about three miles outside of Battle Creek. We met James (Jim) Wright and his family, who lived in Springfield also. Jim and I also worked together in the NATO branch. Jim's wife's name was Mildred, and they had a son Jimmy and a daughter Denise who were around the age of Willis Jr. and Monica. Mildred and Mary established a friendship, and Monica and Denise were very close friends during high school. I believe their friendship helped Monica's transition from St. Louis to the Battle Creek area.

Our family lived in the Battle Creek area for 11 years. I had a very positive work experience during that time. Additionally, Mary was able to accomplish her goal of furthering her nursing education by obtaining her BSN and MNS degrees during the time we lived in Springfield, MI.

I worked in the NATO Cataloging Branch for one year as a GS-9 cataloger. I applied for a job in the Technical Logistics Directorate for the position of the DLA Interchangeability and Substitutability (I&S) program manager. It was a GS-11 position.

The DoD I&S program had strong political implications within the Headquarters, Defense Logistics Agency (DLA). There were high stakes riding on the success of the program for the DLA overall. As the DLSC I&S program manager, I was responsible for assisting with and developing the functional requirements for programmers to design, program, and implement an operational computer database I&S system.

I had been working as the DLSC I&S program manager for about a month, when Mr. Gessner, the director of the Technical and Logistics Directorate, told me that he wanted me to brief the I&S Program to the DLSC commander (an Army colonel) and all the DLSC directors, who were GS-15 grade level. In addition, the DLSC commander's military aide, a US Air Force major, was seated to the right of the commander. I had never briefed at the command level before. In the commander's outer office, while we were waiting for the briefing to start, one director, Mr. Roger Roy, walked up to me and introduced himself as we shook hands. He then said, "You are the guy in the barrel today." As he laughed, he then said, "Don't be nervous. You know more about this program than we do." His comments put me at ease.

The two tables together created a T-shape. There were three directors seated on each side of the table. I was standing at the end of the table, at a podium, facing the DLSC commander and his aide. The briefing took 45 minutes to complete. When I had completed my briefing, there were two exceptional statements made that I still recall today.

The first statement was made by the commander's aide, who said, "I have been assigned to DLSC for three years now, and this, by far, is the best briefing I have heard since I have been here."

The second statement was made by the director of the Cataloging Directorate (I believe his comment to Mr. Gessner was intended to be private.), who asked him, "Where did you get Willis from?"

Smiling, he said, "We promoted him from the Cataloging Directorate." I had started my DLSC career in the NATO Cataloging Division, over which Mr. Chatfield was the director. However, he didn't know who I was.

It's amazing to me that I went from not being selected for the job I should have had initially, to getting a job that allowed me to demonstrate my abilities. If I had been selected for the initial job that Dick Ferrari was selected to fill, I possibly would have not had such an opportunity.

Subsequently, I was promoted into an organization that allowed me to further demonstrate my abilities at the highest level in the DLSC Command, which enabled me to be selected as the DLSC employee of the year. Later I was promoted to a GS-12 position as a result of my visibility as the DLSC I&S program manager. Rhetorically, I always think back to Ma Dear's words, "Just trust in the Lord."

Moving from Battle Creek to Alexandria, Virginia

When DLA field level employees were considered knowledgeable about their program, it was standard practice to recruit them to work at HQ DLA.

Our family had lived in Battle Creek for almost 11 years. At that time, I started to get inquiries about working at the Headquarters (HQ) Defense Logistics Agency (DLA) in Alexandria, VA. My former coworker, Cliff Noaeill, had taken a job at HQ DLA the previous year. He told me how he enjoyed working in the Engineering and Standardization Directorate.

In 1984, I had another opportunity to advance my professional career. I discussed the possibility of moving to HQ DLA with Mary. Mary and I had a similar conversation to the one that we had prior to moving to Battle Creek. The scenario was basically the same—Mary and I discussed the situation, we came to an agreement, and we prayed about what decision we should make.

Mary was eager to make the move. Willis Jr. and Monica had finished high school and started college. They spent almost two years in college, but neither was currently in school. Therefore, Mary encouraged me to accept the job at HQ DLA. Mary was certain she would be able to get a job at the Veterans Administration (VA) in Washington, DC. She had earned her bachelor and master's degrees in nursing from Michigan University at Ann Arbor, MI.

I was well regarded in the Technical Directorate at HQ DLA. I wasn't particularly interested in working in the Cataloging Division. If I went to HQ DLA, I wanted to work in the Engineering and Standardization Division, where I had the knowledge and expertise in the programs in that division.

However, word came from HQ DLA that I should apply for an open position in the Federal Cataloging Division. Then Hank Fillippi could work on getting me moved to the Engineering and Standardization Division. I was heavily recruited to apply for the position that was advertised as a GS-12 with promotion to a GS-13 after one year. That was the normal process when advertising vacancies for job positions at HQ DLA.

I was told that there were several other highly qualified applicants for the cataloging position. Initially, another applicant, who had a PhD, was selected for the position. I don't know if that was the branch chief's choice or not. However, I understand the Cataloging Division Chief overrode that decision and selected me for the job. Accordingly, the Division Chief was the person who hired me.

I understood that personnel hired into HQ DLA would normally be hired at the GS-12 Level with promotion potential to a GS-13 after their first year, and that always did happen. However, I told Mary that I would only accept the job if I was hired as a GS-13.

I was offered a GS-13 position instead of the GS-12 position. Therefore, Mary and I made the decision that I would accept the position at HQ DLA, and we would move to Virginia. Mary and I discussed with Willis Jr., Monica, and Kermit Matthew that we would be moving to Virginia after Kermit's school year was completed.

Overall, the dynamics of this move were different, unlike the move from St. Louis to Battle Creek. Our two oldest children were young adults now, and our youngest son would just be starting high school. Mary had a job with the VA Hospital in Battle Creek, and she was certain that she could work for the VA Hospital in Washington, DC. I had established my Federal Civil Service career in the Defense Logistics Agency, and effectively I had been recruited for the job at HQ DLA.

The physical move of our household furniture and belongings would be handled by a professional moving company. Mary would not have the task of independently packing up the house; I would not have to drive a U-Haul truck to move our belongings to Virginia, as we had done when we moved to Battle Creek.

However, I had to move to Virginia approximately three months before Mary, Monica, and Kermit Matthew would be able to move to Virginia. They had to wait until early June when Kermit was out of school.

I started working in the HQ DLA Cataloging Division in April 1984, and I had to make an adjustment. There was a different approach and attitude at the headquarters level opposed to the DLA field activities. At the headquarters level, policy and procedures were made and guidance was directed to the defense logistics field activities to implement the policies and procedures.

Mary came to Virginia in May to look for housing before we moved the family in June. Not knowing the area, one week was not sufficient to make a decision to buy a house. However, we were able to rent a four-bedroom house located in Burke, VA. It was a nice residential area in the Longwood Knolls community in Burke.

Kermit Matthew enrolled in the Lake Braddock High School. He met Marcus Crockett in our neighborhood, and they became great friends throughout high school. Our daughter Monica married her fiancé, Gordon Zinn, in December 1984, and moved back to Battle Creek. Mary took time to learn the communities in Northern Virginia while looking for a house for us to buy. After four or five months, Mary applied for a job at the Washington, DC, VA Hospital and was hired immediately.

CHAPTER 23

◇

Transfer—Technical, Engineering, and Standardization Division

◇

I HAD TRANSFERRED WITH HIGH expectations of advancing my work career. I was hired by the Cataloging Division Chief, for whom I had a very high regard. I also interacted well with my coworkers in my branch and with others working in the Cataloging Division. Since I already knew many of the people at the HQ DLA, it allowed me to assimilate comfortably into my new work environment.

The only person in the branch I did not have a reasonable rapport with was my branch chief. As an African-American, I did not ascribe to any of his off-tone comments and jokes. I would let him know very specifically when I didn't appreciate his comments. As a result, I think he felt uncomfortable around me.

I had been working at HQ DLA in the Cataloging Division for two months when my branch chief refused to approve my travel (TDY) request to Battle Creek that had been requested by the Technical, Engineering, and Standardization Division Chief. That was the straw that broke the camel's back, figuratively speaking. I knew then that my branch chief had a personal resentment toward me. My travel request had to be elevated to the Senior Executive Service (SES) level for approval. At that point I knew I could not work under that branch chief and enjoy my job and have a successful career.

It seems that every time a crisis was presented to me, a solution was provided. Sometimes it may have been in the form of a guardian angel or a natural recourse. But it always arrived on time.

I desperately needed to change my job so I could build my career at HQ DLA.

Six or seven months after the branch chief had refused to approve my TDY request, a job opening became available in the Technical, Engineering, and Standardization Division for the DoD Interchangeability and Substitutability (I&S) program manager position.

I had a heartfelt conversation with the Cataloging Division Chief who hired me. I wanted him to know that I was going to apply for the DoD I&S program manager position. I had the highest respect for him personally and professionally. He was one of my strongest supporters at HQ DLA. He did not try to dissuade me from leaving the Cataloging Division. He said he completely understood why I wanted to get out of the cataloging branch. He said he didn't want to lose me, but he wished me well with getting the job. With my experience in the program area, It was anticipated that I would be selected for the position.

There was not a promotion involved; it was a straight lateral transfer. However, I was able to get out from under the supervision of the branch chief in the Cataloging Division. There were coworkers with whom I had established strong friendships, including Cynthia Ellison, Gladys Frye, Lois Smith, Tisa Cross-Sadler, and George Baden. My desk was next to John Anderson, a colleague who encouraged me to disregard the branch chief's behavior. There were other friends in the directorate who had also helped me when I arrived at DLA. As much as anyone, my friend Cliff Noaeill helped me get settled in the job. Cliff and his wife Barbara were our good friends. In addition, Sam Burge, Phil Altman, Brenda Scruggs, Etta Dorsey, Claire Arnold, Oscar Grant,

Chauncey Dunham, and many others whose names I don't recall, were all instrumental in helping me assimilate to my new DLA environment.

Working as the DoD I&S program manager was refreshing for me. The change of jobs reinvigorated me personally. I could use my instincts and imagination to improve on the systemic processes that were currently in place for the DoD I&S Program. My association with the service and agency representatives allowed me to create a consensus that was workable for the benefit of the Federal Government overall. Individuals who were paramount in developing the DoD I&S system included: Willard Smith, Barbara Fox, Oscar Grant, Russell (Russ) Parker, Juanita Dunleavy, Teresa Krebs, Richard (Dick) Strang, Pearl Allen, Sam Merritt, Fred Felder, Carl Stites, Sandra Mentry, Deborah Fryar, Kim Leach, Tom Kennedy, Jim H. (I don't recall his last name), Larry Fronzak, Terry Felter, Ken Snader, Doug French, Lyneice Hunter, Wayne Godfrey, Chuck Long, and others.

Working with the DLA field level activities and at the military services made my job easier to implement a DoD I&S system. I basically had autonomy to operate the program independently to get the job done. I was obligated to answer to Hank Fillippi, the division chief. As the DoD I&S program manager, I was able to utilize my knowledge, innovation, and overall skills and abilities in a professional manner.

After Cliff Noaeill retired in 1989 or 1990, I was assigned his responsibilities as the Item Reduction program manager. I then was able to submit an accretion of duty evaluation. I submitted the request to the DLA personnel department to evaluate my job functions for consideration for a GS-14 or GS-15 position.

I had received information to have my job considered for an accretion of duty evaluation from a close friend, Charles Smith, who was a GS-15 and the director of another government agency. Otherwise, I wouldn't have known about the accretion of duty policy.

When I submitted an accretion of duty evaluation, it possibly was the first time that had been done in the directorate. Subsequently, my fellow coworkers asked me what I had done to have my job evaluated. There was another coworker who I advised, and had his GS-13 position upgraded to a GS-14 position.

I recognized the synergy between the DoD I&S and the Item Reduction Programs. I implemented new ideas to cut costs and save money for the Federal Government. I had total support from my coworkers in the division. I can go down a list of personnel who helped me be successful in managing the two programs: Willard Smith, Claire Arnold, Mary Hart, Christine (Chris) Metz, Jean Wiley, Emma Duhart, and Etta Dorsey were outstanding. Tom Ridgway, William (Bill) Finkel, and William (Bill) Lee from the Engineering Branch also supported my work efforts.

Overall, with the support I received from those individuals, I was able to be successful in my job. As a result, our team contributed tremendously to the various DLA initiatives and programs over which I was the program manager. As a program manager, I know our team contributed well to the Department of Defense's mission during my thirty-plus years of Federal Government service.

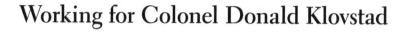

CHAPTER 24

Working for Colonel Donald Klovstad

I AM NOT CERTAIN WHEN Colonel Donald Klostavd, USAF (Col. K) was assigned to the Technical, Engineering, and Standardization Division. He was an air force colonel, and to my knowledge, he was new to DLA.

We worked on several projects together. When we traveled together on TDY (temporary duty), he would arrange excellent accommodations at the officer's quarters. To be eligible for accommodations at the officer's quarters, you had to be a military officer or a grade GS-14 or above.

DPR Program Manager

The first project I worked with Col K on was the defense performance review (DPR) project. It was initiated during the Clinton/Gore presidency, as part of the national performance review. The DPR was the initiative of Vice President Gore's, and it included the various agencies under the Department of Defense, reviewing their programs to improve their operations, and identifying those that should be eliminated. HQ DLA had multiple programs under the DPR initiative, and the Technical and Engineering Division had four programs under the DPR. Initially he assigned two individual program managers in the branch, one DPR initiate each. For some reason, the project was not progressing at the pace Col. K anticipated.

He called me to his office for a meeting. He said, "Drake, I am going to ask you to do something, and you may think it's more than you can handle. However, I was told by people that I have total confidence in that if I wanted to get something done, then I should assign it to Drake. Drake, I know you can get this project completed and done right."

At that point, I was thinking to myself, *What in the world will Col. K come up with now that he wants me to work on?*

He assigned me to work on the DPR project. He said, "Drake, I will give you all the help and support you need. The two program managers I assigned to manage two of the DPR initiates are not getting the job done. Therefore, I want you to manage all four of the DPR projects."

I told him that there was a GS-11 working at DSCC in Columbus, OH, who was trying to get a temporary GS-12 internship at HQs DLA. If he could bring her on board to that position, she would be the only resource I would need to assist me on the project.

Col. K said, "Okay, give me her name and the name of her supervisor, and I will see if I can get her assigned to the internship here at DLA to assist you." I told him her name was Patricia (Patty) Fish.

He also told me that he had assigned three other people under my leadership - a navy lieutenant commander assigned to the DISC (Defense Industrial Supply Center) located in Philadelphia, PA, Mr. Doug Dapo from DSCC (Defense Supply Center Columbus) located in Columbus, OH, to work the wood products project: Ms. Kathy Cutler, from DSCR (Defense Supply Center Richmond), in Richmond, VA, to work the variable pricing project. Col. K emphasized that if I ran into any trouble with the projects, to let him know as soon as I knew. He said we had just about one year to complete the four projects and meet the DPR initiatives of Vice President Gore.

I focused my entire attention on getting the four DPR projects completed on time. Overall, I had about twelve and a half months to complete the project. With the four high-quality individuals assigned to work with me, we were able to complete each of the four projects and the reports on schedule.

The deadline for completing the four DPR projects was only a week away, and we had accumulated all of the required information to write the report. I solicited the help of my friend and one of the best typists, secretaries, and action officers I had worked with, Claire Arnold. She worked in our division, and I could ask her to go beyond the requirements of the job responsibilities and she would. It did not matter if it would take her longer hours. She would do what was required to get the job done. I explained to her that I needed to have all four reports structured in the prescribed format and with the proper report covers by Thursday.

When Thursday morning rolled around, Claire had typed the four individual reports in accordance with my instructions. The day before the reports were to be completed, I informed Col. K that we had completed the DPR project.

He asked, "Which one of the projects were you able to complete?"

I replied, "We completed all four of the DPR projects." I let him know that Claire Arnold had to work late several evenings to type the report for each DPR initiative.

I gave him the four completed typed reports. The wood products project had a green report cover. The variable pricing project had a yellow report cover. The tailored logistics project had a red report cover. The match your price project had a brown report cover. He didn't say anything. He just took the reports and looked at them. It was if he was astonished that I had completed all four of the reports.

I sat in the chair next to his desk. After he finished looking at the one report, he said, "Drake, thanks I knew you would get the job done. I am going to take the reports to Dr. Marshall Bailey so he can submit them to the DLA office that is overseeing the DPR initiatives."

Col. K. later informed me that our Directorate, Supply Management was the first organization within DLA to submit initiatives to the DPR Office for Designation and Reinvention Laboratories. Also, these projects were able to move from concept to execution of the DPR Best Value Common Supplies and Service Initiative.

As a result of that specific DPR project, as well as other work that I had accomplished. I was awarded the DLA Meritorious Civilian Service Award. This award is commonly the second-highest award and medal provided to civilian employees within agencies of the Federal Government of the United States.

After the DPR initiative was completed, Col K assigned me to work on several other DLA cutting-edge projects. I was DLA's representative and a voting member on the CommerceNet team. I believe there were a total of five members who had the voting power on the CommerceNet consortium. Initially, Col K and I traveled together to the first CommerceNet meeting which I think was held in Palo Alto or San Jose, CA. I don't recall if it was on the Stanford University campus or not.

At the first meeting Col. K introduced me to the founder/cofounder of CommerceNet, Jay (Marty) Tenenbaum, and the other committee members. He informed Marty that I would be the DLA representative and my vote and decisions would be final. Every month for three years I would fly into San Francisco, CA., to attend the three-day CommerceNet meetings. I represented DLA's interest at the meetings by providing expertise (a voice) to help shape what would become the "industry standards" regarding the transaction protocol and procedures for operating the internet.

Also I was the connection to the DLA R&D (research and development) program and how the government (DLA) would interface with using the internet. As a result, I worked closely with Don O'Brien, Julie Tsao, Dan Gearing, Ken Urtel, Tony Monteleone, John Christensen, and periodically the senior executive service (SES) R&D director, Scottie Knott.

I was part of the DLA team that initially worked with incorporating Partnet capabilities and technology into the DLA online e-commerce opportunities. During the early years, I traveled with Dr. Don Brown of Partnet going to various DLA agencies and other entities to demonstrate and inform the DLA Supply Centers about Partnet. I remember in the following years that Debra (Debby) Fryar was a Partnet program manager when she worked at DLSC. There were other DLA employees whose names I can't recall who were involved in the Partnet effort within DLA.

CHAPTER 25

$\diamond$

Retired from DLA and Federal Government

$\diamond$

I RETIRED FROM THE DEFENSE Logistics Agency in January 2001, after completing 33 years of Federal service. By most standards, I had a complete, fulfilling, and successful work career. Moreover, if I include the seven years I worked on the GSA government contract, I would have spent 40 years working for the Federal Government, directly and indirectly. I was able to earn a sufficient livelihood for my family as a Federal Civil Service employee. Even more so, I provided my country with resolute service during my Federal career, and I am proud of my contribution to my country as a civil servant.

As I prepared to exit from my Federal career, I paused and reflected in retrospect on the fact that during my 30-year career, I encountered attitudes and behavior of individuals in the workplace that was a microcosm of our overall society in general. I had a wonderful experience with people who were decent, hardworking individuals who had common interests with me. Their values were centered on fair play, treating people right, and having a core value of what's right as human beings. Conversely, I encountered some not-so-fair-minded people. Their attitudes and behavior were outright obstinate and against the norm of what was right and fair to other individuals. However, they were in the minority.

I believe the right people were placed in my life at the exact right time who allowed me to have some success during my work career. I know I didn't accomplish what I did, regardless of how small, without the Lord God Almighty and his purpose for my life.

I had formally established Male Duck, Incorporated (MDI) in 1988. I didn't start operating MDI until I had officially retired from the Federal Government. When I retired in January 2001, I was able to move into my role as executive vice president of MDI.

My father passed away on August 4, 1989. However, before he passed, I was able to discuss with my father that I had established MDI and my plans to have a family business. I don't recall specifically what my father's reaction was at that point. He was mentally alert, but he wasn't able to verbalize his thoughts since he was incapacitated from a stroke. I could clearly see on his face that he was pleased that I had established MDI. By that time, my father knew that my two older brothers Charles and Kermit Jr., had gone into business for themselves for a short time.

I was looking forward to starting my second career. During the years before I retired, I consulted with the DLA attorney, Walter, to avoid any conflicts of interest that would have prevented me from getting involved with operating MDI while I was working. Again, Mary and I were still being blessed. God is good!

When I retired, I was ready and able to become totally involved in MDI's day-to-day business operations. I still needed a challenge to stay active for the next three years until my wife, Mary, retired from her job at the VA Hospital. Then we could start traveling and enjoy our retirement lives.

CHAPTER 26

$\diamond$

Operating MDI (Male Duck, Incorporated)

$\diamond$

T HE CREATION OF MDI STARTED in my spirit, mind, and inspiration. Actually, it started in concept when I was 14 or 15 years old. It was a weekend. My father told me he wanted me to take a ride with him in his old truck, a black, enclosed truck with a few gray stripes on the side panels.

I didn't know where my father was taking me. It wasn't often that my dad and I rode in the truck unless we were going to Soulard Farmer's Market in south St, Louis on a Saturday to pick up produce from the open market. Dad said he wanted to show me something as we continued driving toward downtown St. Louis.

When we got to downtown St. Louis, Dad continued driving. He crossed over the Eads Bridge to East Saint Louis, IL, and pulled up in front of a vacant building. I think it was located on Broadway and Fourth Streets. We didn't get out of the truck, but my father started explaining what he saw as the potential for a very good business opportunity.

I believe my father saw in me what could be the lynchpin to make his vision happen. It may have been because of my work ethic and how I got things done as a kid. After he had shared his vision with me about this potential opportunity, he said, "I don't see why you and your brothers don't put your money together and buy this building. You can start a Laundromat business. You could pay off the loan in a short time." If I could read my dad's mind, I could hear him saying, "If only I had the chance when I was your age. I would be able to take care of my family in the right way."

Then my father said, "I just wanted to show you the idea that I had. Son, I know it will work, and you can make a lot of money if you'll work together. I talked to the lady who owns the building. Her husband recently died, and she wants to sell the property. The building needs some repairs, but we could do most of the work ourselves. We probably can get the lady to hold the loan and we wouldn't have to go to a bank for a loan."

Dad started the truck and we headed back across the bridge, returning home to St Louis. During the ride home, my father said, "There is not a Laundromat business in East Saint Louis. People are looking for some place where they can wash and dry their clothes."

After that day, my father and I would periodically talk about that building. However, within a month, my father told me that the owner had sold the building.

That discussion I had with my father was in 1954 or 1955. It was the initial motivation that I had to start a family business. Both of my brothers started their own businesses. Kermit Jr. had started several janitorial service companies when he lived in California and also in Memphis, TN. His businesses had a level of success, but Kermit Jr. didn't let the company mature, and ultimately closed the business after a few years. Likewise, my brother Charles started several businesses, and he did not allow his businesses to fully develop.

As a young adult living in S. Louis, I didn't have a primary interest in starting a business. I was focused on getting a job so I could buy our first house. We were blessed to buy our first home nine years after Mary and I were married. We were able to save enough money to pay cash for our house; instead, we got a loan from the bank against our savings and paid off our mortgage in three years.

Then I had thoughts of starting a business. The conversation I had with my father years ago never completely left my consciousness. My first plan was to start a lawn service business. I wanted to set up my nephew Wayne Gooch, who was old enough to drive a truck, with my son Willis Jr. and my nephew Stephone Cody to operate the business.

I would purchase a truck, lawn mowers, and any other equipment needed for the lawn service business. It would be their business. I envisioned that Wayne could drop Willis Jr. and Stephone at the houses where they had lawns to cut. It was the summer of 1974 when I planned to start the business for them. I had discussed this with my father, and he too thought it was a good idea. They could also earn money for the summer. However, before I could implement my idea and start the business, I got a job in Battle Creek, MI. Our family moved from St. Louis that summer, so that opportunity never materialized.

Interestingly enough, when I moved to Battle Creek in 1974, I discarded the thoughts of starting a business. Again, I was focused on getting settled in the new area where we were living. I had to focus on learning a new job and getting our family situated in our new home. It was close to nine or ten years before I again started thinking about starting a business.

I officially established MDI as a bona fide corporation, registered in the state of Michigan. However, in 1984 I moved to HQ DLA and didn't pursue operating MDI as a business in Battle Creek.

My father suggestion to me that his four sons should start a laundromat business still resonated with me after 32 years. I still had the mind-set of establishing a family business. I wanted to try to accomplish my father's dream that his four sons would establish a family business. His dream became an initiative for me, and I established MDI (Male Duck Incorporated) as a registered corporation in the state of Virginia in 1988. When I retired from Federal Civil Service in 2001, I became involved in MDI's day-to-day operation with the establishment of a Federal Government consulting business.

The business was named Male Duck Incorporated as a translation of our surname, Drake, which is, interestingly enough, a male duck. MDI was successfully launched with the award of our first government contract in 2001.

MDI was operated mainly by the president, Kermit Matthew Drake; the executive vice president, Willis Drake (me); and the secretary-treasurer and office manager, Mary Ann Byas-Drake. The day-to-day operation of MDI was managed by the executive vice president. MDI is an 8a certified company and has a GSA Mission Oriented Business Integrated Services (MOBIS) contract entering into its thirtieth year of existence.

During the peak years of operations, MDI employed 16 personnel located in eight states (Virginia, Ohio, New York, Chicago, Georgia, Pennsylvania, Florida, and New Jersey). MDI created a reputation of completing its assignments on time and fulfilling its contracts within budget and with a very high level of success.

Over the years MDI was staffed with high quality personnel with a combined work experience in excess of 100 years in the field of R&D and Logistics; namely, Don O'Brien, Dan Gearing, Ken Urtel, John Cesarone, Michael Stets, William (Bill) Christy, Diana Cross, William (Bill) Finkel, Bernie Johns, Kathy Moore, Hunter Meadows, Paul Grover and others. Their expertise allowed MDI to provide excellent service to our customers.

Over time MDI was able to bid on and was awarded contracts totaling in the millions of dollars. My hourly labor rate was reasonable at $174 an hour. The fact that I could earn $174 an hour from where I started at $1 an hour is evidence of my blessings.

I know it is proof or a testament that MDI operated as a bona fide small business that the Federal Government depended on for excellent services. MDI hired outstanding consultants for the various contracts it supported. Additionally, I am certain that the business opportunities MDI received were due in part to the corporate expertise and the reputation I had established over my extensive thirty-plus years of working as a Federal civil servant during my career. I possess organic corporate expertise within the DLA, as well as knowledge of the four major military services' modes of operations.

I still remember that ride over to East Saint Louis, IL, when my father planted that seed of possibility; a dream that I was able to make into a reality.

Acknowledgments

I want to express my love and appreciation to my late, beloved wife, Mary Ann Byas-Drake, who was also affectionately known as Pookie. During our fifty-five wonderful years of marriage, Mary and I were spiritually connected. I know that God blessed Mary, me, and our family more than I can imagine we deserved. My love goes out to my son Willis L. Drake Jr.; my daughter, Monica Renee Drake-Zinn; my son Kermit Matthew Drake; and my grandchildren and great-grandchildren.

I am thankful to each of my siblings who provided their support for me to write this book, my story: Melvin Drake, Shirley Ethel Drake-Sykes, Jean Lois Drake, and Joan Louise Drake-Harris.

I want to acknowledge the friendships I developed growing up in our small community that essentially encompassed Taylor Avenue at Enright, Finney, Fairfax, and Cook Avenues. Those friendships were monumental in helping me become the person I am today. During my childhood, I had so many guardian angels watching over me. I know my life was enriched by the friendships of James Anderson, Stanley McKissic, Arthur (Al) Buford, Frank Perkins, Francis Hutchinson, James Hutchinson, Norman Anderson, and Cleart Jones, all of whom lived in the immediate neighborhood, including my elementary schoolmates Oree Armstrong, Elgin Walker, Annette Williams, Frank Saunders, James Whitfield, and others.

I'd also like to recognize my mother, Wylor Dean Sanford-Drake; my father, Kermit Drake; my aunt Ethel Mae Sanford (Tee); my great-uncle Jesse Smith; Mrs. Mae Carter-Layne; my late sister, Maudean

Drake-Gill; and my late brothers Charles Edward Drake and Kermit Drake Jr.

I want to thank an associate and friend, Honorable William (Bill) Clay, former representative for Missouri's first district, for encouraging me to tell my story and write this book.

I want to thank two unnamed persons (and they know who they are) that were invaluable to me during the early stages of editing my manuscript. Their support encouraged me to tell my story in a published book.

Claire Arnold has been a friend to Mary and I for 30 years. I reached out to her for help in editing my manuscript and, at the final hour, without hesitation, she answered my call. I want to thank her from the bottom of my heart for her excellent help and support in editing my book.

Appendix

Drake vs. Hicks

Annotate this Case

249 S.W.2d 358 (1952)

DRAKE et al. v. HICKS et al.

No. 42778.

Supreme Court of Missouri, Division No. 2.

June 9, 1952.

Witherspoon, Lewis & Draper, St. Louis, for appellants.

William C. Connett, IV, Thomas V. Connelly, St. Louis (Bryan, Cave, McPheeters & McRoberts, St. Louis, of counsel), for respondents.

*359 BENNICK, Judge.

This is a suit for the specific performance of a contract to convey certain real estate known as 4460-62 Enright Avenue, in the City of St. Louis.

The plaintiffs are Kermit Drake and Wylor Dean Drake, his wife, the prospective purchasers of the property. The principal defendant is Fred Hicks, the owner of the property. The other defendants, Willie Joe Parker and Frankie Matthews, are the persons named as lessees in certain purported leases which the court found to have been executed by Hicks, not in good faith, but for the purpose of aiding him in avoiding the terms of his contract.

On September 9, 1950, Hicks entered into a written contract for the sale of the property to plaintiffs for the total sum of $12,000, of which $300 was thereby receipted for as earnest money; the sum of $8,700 was to be paid in cash upon the closing of the sale; and the remaining $3,000 was to be evidenced by notes of $90 each, payable monthly, bearing interest at 6% per annum, and secured by a second deed of trust which was to be subject to an outstanding first deed of trust for $7,500.

The contract further provided that the sale was to be closed on or before October 2, 1950, at the real estate office of Oreon E. Scott in St. Louis, and that time was to be of the essence of the contract.

Hicks and the Drakes had previously arranged to meet in Scott's office on September 9th for the preparation of the necessary papers in confirmation of the oral agreement that had been reached between them; and it was Scott who drew the contract and accepted and retained the deposit of the earnest money. Scott had agreed to undertake the financing for the Drakes, but, according to his version of the transaction, did not otherwise purport to act as agent for either party.

The deal was of course not closed on or before October 2nd as had been provided by the contract; and the principal question in the lower court was which of the parties was responsible for the failure of performance. Plaintiffs' evidence was to the effect that Hicks had theretofore announced his repudiation of the contract, and that it was because of such fact, and in reliance upon advice from Scott, that plaintiffs did not appear at Scott's office on the day fixed for the closing of the deal. Hicks denied that he had ever told plaintiffs or anyone else that he would not go through with the sale, but insisted, on the contrary, that not only had he been at all times ready and willing to carry out his part of the transaction, but that he had in fact waited for plaintiffs outside Scott's office during the whole of the afternoon of October 2nd.

Even though plaintiffs did not appear at Scott's office on October 2nd, they did go there on October 3rd and completed the arrangements for financing the transaction. However Hicks was then unwilling to close the deal, and this suit for specific performance followed.

There is no question in the case regarding the sufficiency of the pleadings, of which it is enough to say that they set out the facts in substantially the same fashion as they have heretofore appeared in our own statement of the case.

The court took the case under advisement, and in due time entered an interlocutory finding and decree that plaintiffs were entitled to specific performance, provided they should comply with their own obligations under the contract; and that if, within 10 days, they would deposit with the clerk the amount to be paid in cash together with "second deed of trust and notes as called for under the terms of the sales contract", the court would then order that title be passed.

Thereafter the court entered a final decree in which, having found that plaintiffs had meanwhile complied with the provisions of the interlocutory order by a deposit of cash and "notes secured by second deed of trust as called for in the terms of the sales contract", the court adjudged that title be divested out of defendant Hicks and be vested in plaintiffs subject to the liens of the first and second deeds of trust.

Within due time defendants filed their motion for a new trial in which they set up, among other things, that the court had erred in rendering such final decree for the reason *360 that plaintiffs had not in fact complied with the terms of the interlocutory decree.

The motion being overruled, defendants gave notice of appeal, and by proper successive steps have caused the case to be transferred to this court for its review.

Inasmuch as a case of this character involves title to real estate within the meaning of Art. V, Sec. 3, Constitution of 1945, V.A.M.S., appellate jurisdiction is vested in this court. State ex rel. Place v. Bland, 353 Mo.

639, 183 S.W.2d 878; Barnes v. Stone, 198 Mo. 471, 478, 95 S.W. 915; Herzog v. Ross, Mo. App., 192 S.W.2d 23.

While the three defendants joined in the appeal, the points for decision are all confined to matters in controversy between Hicks and plaintiffs.

There is no merit in the suggestion that specific performance should have been denied upon the ground that the contract for the sale of the property was uncertain, indefinite, and incomplete in its essential terms. On the contrary, its provisions were amply sufficient to warrant a decree that they be carried out. Herzog v. Ross, 355 Mo. 406, 196 S.W.2d 268, 167 A.L.R. 407; Rayburn v. Atkinson, Mo. Sup., 206 S.W.2d 512; Henleben v. Krause, Mo. Sup., 209 S.W.2d 888.

As a matter of fact, Hicks' real complaint is not that the contract was uncertain, indefinite, and incomplete, but rather that plaintiffs themselves did not comply with those provisions of the contract which were conditions precedent to the right to compel performance by him. To be precise, he insists that the notes and the second deed of trust which were tendered by plaintiffs in purported obedience to the interlocutory decree were not such as were required by the terms of the contract, and that the court was consequently in error in entering a final decree for specific performance upon the theory of compliance on the part of plaintiffs.

There are two propositions that are fundamental in the law of specific performance. The one is that the court will not make a contract for the parties, and that if it undertakes to enforce their own contract, it will require the performance of neither more nor less than that which the parties themselves have agreed to do. Baldwin v. Corcoran, 320 Mo. 813, 7 S.W.2d 967; Rayburn v. Atkinson, supra. The other is that the party who seeks relief must show his performance or offer of performance of every essential obligation resting upon him before the other party may be compelled to perform. Parkhurst v. Lebanon Publishing Co., 356 Mo. 934, 204 S.W.2d 241; Long v. Rogers, Mo. App., 185 S.W.2d 863.

It will be recalled that by the provisions of the contract plaintiffs were required, among other things, to execute notes aggregating $3,000 but of the face amount of $90 each, payable monthly, bearing interest at the rate of 6%, and secured by a second deed of trust.

In contemplation of the closing of the deal the notes and deed of trust were executed in Scott's office on September 26th, quite some time after the signing of the contract, and shortly before the day fixed for the completion of the transaction. The notes were 36 in number, the first 35 for $90 each, and the 36th for $139.80. However instead of being made payable to Hicks to whom the money would have been owing, the notes were made payable to one John F. Schrontz, a straw party whose name Scott elected to use for some unexplained reason. Schrontz was also named as third party in the deed of trust; and the plan seems to have been for Schrontz, the ostensible payee, to endorse the notes to Hicks without recourse. The deed of trust had previously been filed for record; and after the entry of the interlocutory order the deed of trust and series of 36 notes were tendered into court in purported compliance with the order, and were found by the court to have been notes and a deed of trust "as called for in the terms of the sales contract".

For his first objection Hicks complains of the inclusion in the deed of trust of a provision granting plaintiffs the privilege of paying the indebtedness secured by such deed of trust in full or in part at any time upon notice to Scott, the trustee, with interest to cease on the principal amount so paid from the date of such principal payment.

*361 Inasmuch as the contract had been made for the benefit, not only of plaintiffs, the purchasers, but also of Hicks, the vendor, the latter had the undoubted right to insist upon strict compliance with the provision for a deferred interest-bearing payment of a portion of the purchase price; and the court was consequently in error in holding that such provision had been satisfied by the tender of a deed of trust containing a prepayment privilege such as was inserted in the deed of trust in question. Baldwin v. Corcoran, supra; Terry v. Michalak, 319 Mo. 290, 3 S.W.2d 701.

A second and perhaps more serious objection is directed at the arrangement whereby the notes and deed of trust were executed in favor of Schrontz, the straw party, instead of in favor of Hicks to whom plaintiffs would have been indebted in the event of performance of the contract. There was nothing in the transaction to cause plaintiffs to become indebted to Schrontz; and the notes and deed of trust which falsely purported to evidence such indebtedness were therefore void for want of consideration, and not of a character which Hicks was bound to accept.

A copy of the deed of trust which plaintiffs tendered into court in purported compliance with the interlocutory order has been transmitted to this court and deposited with the files. Indeed there is no question but that the deed of trust and the notes which it secured contained the particular matters of which Hicks complains. Nor can it be said that the objections he raises are mere afterthoughts, and that there was no preservation of his points in the motion for a new trial. On the contrary, he set up, as we have already indicated, that the court was in error in entering its final decree for the reason that plaintiffs had not complied with the terms of the interlocutory order, which terms were that the court would decree specific performance if plaintiffs would deposit with the clerk, within 10 days, a second deed of trust and notes "as called for under the terms of the sales contract". While plaintiffs deposited the notes and deed of trust well within the designated period, the trouble was that in the two material respects pointed out they were not such notes and deed of trust as were called for by the contract.

It follows that the judgment of the circuit court should be reversed and the cause remanded with directions to the court to reinstate its interlocutory decree as the basis for such further proceedings consistent with the views herein expressed as the facts and circumstances may require. It is so ordered.

All concur

Definitions

1. Restrictive Covenant: A covenant imposing a restriction on the use of land so that the value and enjoyment of adjoining land will be preserved.

2. Restrictive Covenant Law and Legal Definition. A restrictive covenant is a clause in a deed to real property that the buyer (grantee) will be limited as to the future use of the property. All restrictive covenants based on race are illegal.

About the Author

Willis L. Drake, a native of Memphis, Tennessee, was raised in St. Louis, Missouri, and graduated from Sumner High School in 1958. He became a first-time author at the age of seventy-eight. Other than the grace of God, he had no formal training to prepare him to write this book, which he wrote after the death of his wife of fifty-five years, Mary Ann Byas-Drake. Her spirit is always with him.

CPSIA information can be obtained
at www.ICGtesting.com
Printed in the USA
LVHW030744130919
630961LV00006B/70